AF340657

A History of Peirce Junior College, 1865-1989

Carl Fassl

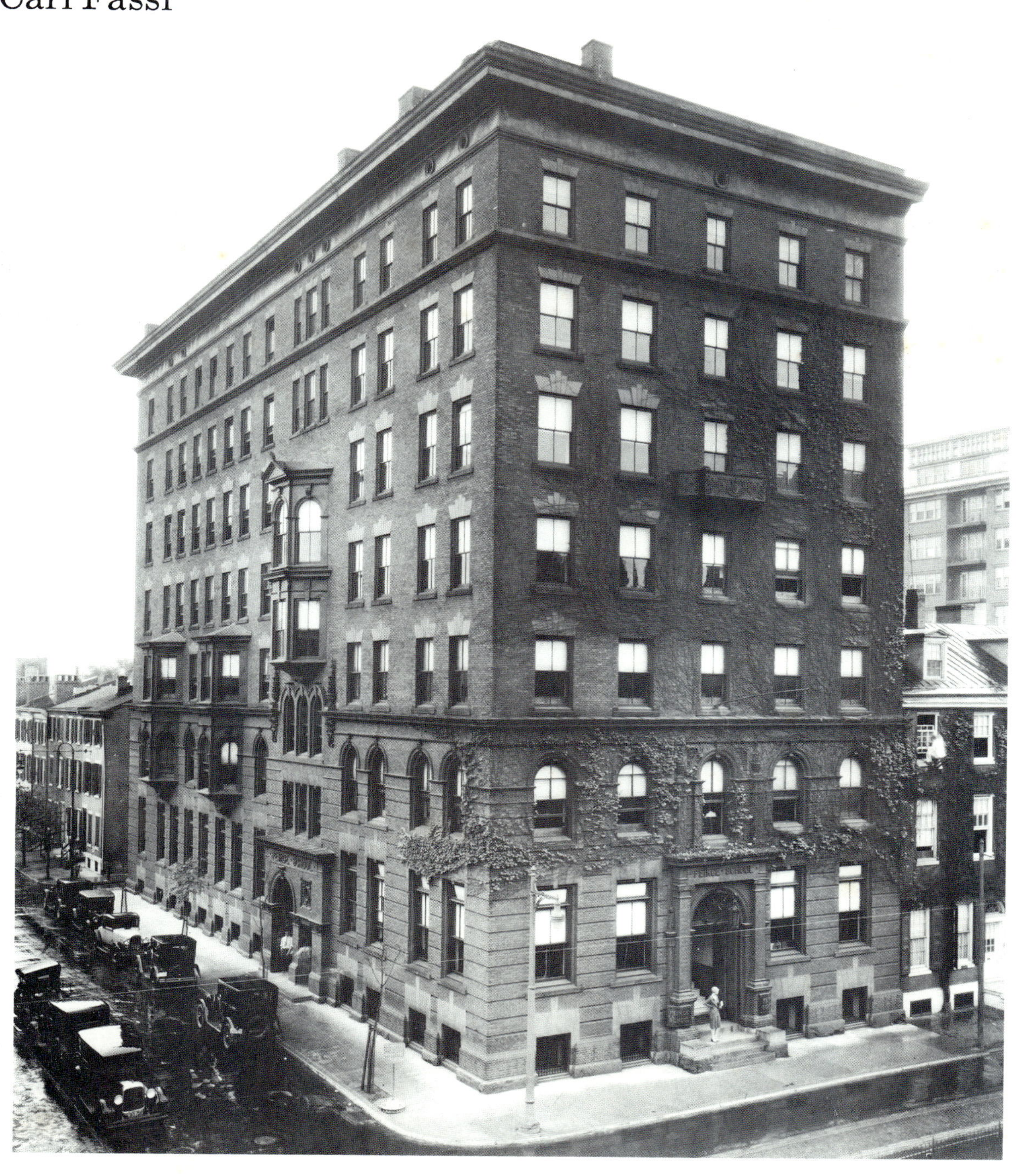

PEIRCE MEANS BUSINESS

A History of Peirce Junior College, 1865-1989

Carl Fassl

First Edition
Philadelphia, 1990
Peirce Junior College

PEIRCE MEANS BUSINESS
A History of Peirce Junior College, 1865 - 1989

Design and Layout by Carlisle Associates and
Intergalactic Publishing Company
Printed by: Maxwell Graphic Arts, Inc.
Gibbsboro, NJ

Library of Congress Cataloging in Publication Data

Fassl, Carl, 1951-

Main entry under title: Peirce Means Business,
A History of Peirce Junior College, 1865 - 1989

1. Colleges. 2. Business Schools. 3 History; Education.
I. Peirce Junior College
II. Library of Congress Catalog Card Number (LCC) 90-60386
ISBN 0-962501-0-9

For Lynda

Contents

The college owes a debt of gratitude to those who so generously contributed to the support of this publication. Without them, the history of Peirce could not have been produced.

Our thanks to the following foundations, companies, and friends:

The Arcadia Foundation; Continental Bank; The Eden Foundation; Hatfield Quality Meats, Inc.; Maxwell Graphic Arts, Inc.; Mylotte, David, and Fitzpatrick; The Walsh Company; The William Goldman Foundation; Anthony J. D'Angelo; William J. Carey; Robert C. Garofola; Hugh Kenworthy, Jr.; Raymond C. Lewin; Charles F. Marshall III; Reverend Robert H. Peoples; J. Richard Uberti; Kathleen Webb; Mark W. Whitehead; and Charles J. Young.

And to the following alumni:

Viola Gill Guté '17; Lawrence R. Zerfing '17; Earl W. Glazier, Sr. '22; George L. Shipps '27; Lillian Guest '31; Thomas May Peirce III '32; Howard L. Buhman '33; J. Linford Snyder '33; George H. Eakle '34; John T. Welsh '34; Gordon H. Freas '36; V. Thelma Snyder '36; Carolyn Tice '36; Albert J. Tordella '36; Harry L. Willits '38; C. Anthony Ricca '39; Dorothy T. Ballinger '40; David L. Simpson '40; W. Herbert Webster '40; Albert G. Cederstrom, Jr. '43; Robert K. Beach '48; Edward Papazian '49; Richard Boorse '50; Harold Barndt '52; Raymond L. Palzer '52; Edwin D. Dewees '61; Joseph P. Tamney '70; and John Bolte '77.

Acknowledgments

I would like to extend my gratitude to the many members of the Peirce Junior College community whose work, interest, and support contributed to the production of this book. Among these, special thanks are due President Raymond C. Lewin, Assistant Dean Mark Whitehead, Director of Library Services Debra Schrammel, and research assistant Yvonne Moss.

Additionally, I wish to thank Dr. Rodney Carlisle and Loretta Carlisle of Rutgers University. Credit for book design should be directed to Sam Valenza and Bonnie Hoffman of Intergalactic Publishing Company.

Finally, I would be remiss not to mention the efforts of several generations of unofficial and unnamed Peirce historians who, by carefully preserving evidence of the past, have made this present work possible.

This book was produced under contract with Peirce Junior College. Except where noted, all narrative and pictorial elements have been drawn from materials on permanent deposit in the Peirce Junior College Archives. Under these circumstances, I have decided against the use of repetitive footnotes. Anyone interested in following up on the material presented here may find the sources of all points of fact in the Peirce Junior College Archives.

Carl Fassl
October, 1989

The Harrison Building, also known as Handel and Haydn Hall, was the first home of the Union Business College. This 1865 sketch depicts the building's long Eighth Street frontage, including the school business office immediately south of the main entrance on the first floor.

Chapter 1

The Founding of the Union Business College

Slightly before nine o'clock on a bright, autumn morning, September 19, 1865, Thomas May Peirce strode the length of the cavernous hall on the second floor of the Harrison Building, Eighth and Spring Garden Streets, in Philadelphia, his footfalls echoing like pistol shots through the empty room.

Peirce paused, one last time, to check his arrangements. The triple rows of wide countinghouse desks and the oaken facade of a bank window which Peirce had installed could not diminish the former music hall's elegance of dimension and bearing. With a high, ornately figured ceiling, heavy globed chandeliers, and richly gilded curtains, the room was unlike any schoolroom Peirce had had occasion to open during his seven year teaching career in Philadelphia's public schools. But then, none of them, and few schools anywhere, were exactly like this one. Peirce resumed his walk, descended a wide, carpeted staircase to ground level, and opened the doors of the Union Business College to students for the first time.

The Harrison Building, a long, ornate, three-story structure, had been built at mid-century as a music hall, presenting a rousing fare of German musicals for both Philadelphia's native and growing immigrant population. As the country moved into the grim era of Civil War, however, the facility's large second-floor hall more often witnessed bitter, sometimes violent, political rallies than music festivals. In September, 1865, barely five months after hostilities had finally ended with the surrender of General Robert E. Lee's rebel forces at Appomatox, most Philadelphians referred to the Harrison Building by the name it had sported in previous peaceful times, Handel and Haydn Hall.

Dr. Peirce, who later received the doctorate in Law and Letters from Dickinson College, had reason to be proud of his new enterprise and its arrangements. Union Business College occupied the entire main hall on the second floor of the building, as well as additional rooms for the ladies department and other special courses on the third and fourth floors. Flickering gas jets illuminated the classrooms on cloudy days and in the evenings, a welcome modern improvement over candles and whale-oil fired lamps. Open fireplaces and "base burning" stoves provided heating. During school hours, the theater chairs in the main hall would be removed to make room for desks. However, the stage and gallery remained, allowing the pragmatic Dr. Peirce to continue to rent the hall for musical performances in the evenings. As it turned out, in the first years, concerts by a Signor Blitz became one of the more popular attractions.

Many historians view the Civil War as a watershed in American history for its role in stimulating industry and setting the stage for the golden age of the American industrial revolution which unfolded in the following decades. Equipping the vast Union and Confederate armies required the production of textiles and armaments in quantities far surpassing the abilities of current, largely artisanal manufacturing technology. The staggering demand for war-related products prompted pioneering efforts in standardized, high-output production, and profits from government contracts during the war years provided the financial basis for many of the post-war industrial powerhouses.

Views of the Union Business College circa 1865. The photo (above) shows the stage and boxes of Handel and Haydn Hall; (at right), the rear of the room and gallery. In both photos, Dr. Peirce is visible standing in the left background.

The main classroom of the Union Business College had originally been designed as a music hall. The drawing (below right), captures the elegance of the room's appointments. Note the ornately sculpted chandeliers and figured ceiling. Fittingly, the School Bank, the cornerstone of Dr. Peirce's Practical Business Department, occupied center stage in the renovated hall.

Pierce's
Union Business College
Philadelphia
Sketched
Specimen of
Pen-Work
Designed for Thomas M. Pierce
as a sample of original Pen-Drawing.
By
Packard
HUMBUG
1875

Peirce had established the school, seeing an opportunity for a new kind of education in the post Civil War years. He was convinced that the growth of Northern manufacturing during the war would fuel unprecedented prosperity with the reopening of Southern markets. Manufacturing meant jobs, not only on the shop floor, but in offices of the factories themselves and the growing network of financial institutions and mercantile houses that arose almost daily to serve them. Loss of life on American battlefields had been appallingly heavy, and while attrition shrank the size of the nation's work force, industrial and commercial expansion provided thousands of new job openings.

Nineteenth-century "penmen" enjoyed an informal fraternity, often gathering extensive collections of samples of each others' work. The drawing (facing page) is an unusually elaborate example of this practice executed for Dr. Pierce by Herbert Packard of Boston in 1873.

"The penmen of UBC will also design and execute ornamental work such as charters, petitions, resolutions, rolls, diplomas, visiting and wedding cards, and invitations for a fee if desired."

At first, Peirce worked with three partners, who would share in the administrative and teaching duties in the new school. In the first months, the other partners, together with Peirce, constituted the faculty, the ownership, and the board of directors simultaneously. In early 1865, Peirce had entered a partnership with three like-minded acquaintances, Chester N. Farr, Jr., an accomplished penman and penmanship instructor; R. D. Carll, a local businessman; and Carll's brother, A. F. Carll, a mathematician. Pooling their resources and talents, the new partners bent to the various tasks of getting their new school off the ground: finding a suitable location, planning curriculum, and composing, printing, and circulating catalogs and advertisements.

In accordance with the tenets of sound business practice that he and the partners proposed to teach, the activities of the Union Business College were divided into four departments. Under the arrangement, each partner had defined duties and responsibilities. The core of the school's curriculum, the business program, comprised the Commercial Department and was under the control of Peirce himself. The Mathematical Department, which offered such courses as Engineering and Surveying as well as Algebra, Geometry, and Trigonometry, came under the auspices of A. F. Carll. Farr handled the penmanship instruction. R. D. Carll managed the business affairs of the firm and staffed the office. The partnership would not last out the year, however. The two Carlls left in November of 1865, and Thomas May Peirce's own father, Caleb F. Peirce, temporarily assumed the operation of the business office.

The Peirce Family Crest

Through Peirce's work as a consulting accountant, as well as his social ties in the Philadelphia business community, he knew that the demand for competent office workers far outstripped the supply. "I knew from business men that advertisements for help were answered by hundreds, and that cases were rare in which more than one per cent. of the applications rose to the dignity of consideration. I did not have money, but I had time, I had youth, and I had some degree of courage, and I gave myself to the work of training the ninety-nine percent of applicants who wanted to go into business and whose previous preparation did not secure for them even consideration at the hands of an employer."

Although only 27 years of age, Peirce was particularly well prepared and positioned when he opened the Union Business College. As a descendant of two of the oldest family lines in Pennsylvania, the Peirces and the Mays, his background lent him the credibility and respect in the local community that came with social standing. Moreover, both families had gained an identity with education. Both Peirce's father, Caleb Peirce, and maternal grandfather, the Reverend Thomas Potts May, had earned respect through long and distinguished careers in teaching.

Early in his career, Dr. Peirce was a candidate for a teaching position. The Board of Directors to whom he applied expressed satisfaction in his teaching credentials, but said that they preferred a married man for the position. Hearing this, the resolute Peirce addressed the board: "Gentlemen, I am informed that you object to my appointment because I am a single man. If you will adjourn this meeting for twenty-four hours I will remove this objection." On December 25, 1861, Thomas May Peirce married Mary Bisbing, apparently gaining at once a job as well as a family.

Peirce's establishment of the Union Business College, which combined an entrepreneurial spirit with a zeal for education, might have been influenced by the career of his father. Caleb Peirce combined vocations successfully and profitably as a journalist, manufacturer, and educator. In addition to teaching, the elder Peirce published the quarterly Newspaper Register from offices at 46 South Third Street, and was for many years the only supplier of printing ink in Philadelphia. The Register, which listed names and addresses of newspapers nationwide as a resource for potential advertisers, often also contained essays as lead stories. Thomas May Peirce was active and interested in his father's work. In 1851, "Master" T. M. Peirce, at age thirteen, was listed as editor of the paper.

Peirce achieved an A.B. degree from Central High School in 1853, and received an A.M. degree from the same institution five years later. (The Master of Arts in the mid-nineteenth century context was not the equivalent of a modern graduate degree. As used at that time, the term described a certificate earned upon completion of secondary work.) After a brief period of self-examination and travel, which included a failed wood engraving enterprise, Peirce settled into a career as an educator. Peirce quickly acquired the reputation as an excellent and dedicated teacher, one who took personal interest and pride in the development of his students.

Peirce particularly displayed these qualities as principal of the Mount Vernon Grammar School in Philadelphia. One measure of a grammar school principal in those days was the percentage of one's graduating class passing the final examination for advancement to high school. Principal Peirce went to extreme lengths to achieve Mount Vernon's virtually unblemished record. In order to prepare students for the high school entrance examination, Peirce annually sequestered himself and the graduating class in the school building to study, sleeping and taking all meals there, for periods of up to six weeks at a time. Peirce's pedantic thoroughness and self-dedication earned him respect among the local educational community that helped pave the way for his success at the Union Business College.

H. W. Flickinger, penmanship instructor at Peirce College of Business, executed a pen and ink portrait of Dr. Peirce (facing page) in 1882.

Sayings of Thomas May Peirce:

"These faculty meetings are open and above board."

"Let me see your string of fish and if it is a better-looking string than mine, I want to learn of you and change my methods."

THOMAS MAY PEIRCE, M.A.,
— PRINCIPAL. —

Early in 1865, working with his partners, Peirce, then principal of the Monroe Public School at Tenth and Buttonwood Streets, leased the second floor of Handel and Haydn Hall to house the Union Business College. The building was owned at that time by the Hand in Hand Company, one of Philadelphia's early insurance organizations. The Hand in Hand Company used the first floor as an engine house to house its fire fighting equipment. Apparently the nickname "Handel and Haydn Hall" was a local clever twist on the name of the insurance company which owned the building.

So it was that on September 18, 1865, the firm of Carll, Peirce, and Farr opened for business in a small office, 531 North Eighth Street, on the ground floor of Handel and Haydn Hall. Nine students: Samuel K. Lenoir, Joseph Dailey, Walter Crowell, James Townsend, William Hulseman, George Ballenger, Henry Harrison, Albert Keyser, and Isadore Coons, registered that day, and attended an informal reception hosted by Peirce that evening. The next morning, September 19, 1865, they became the first students ever to attend the Union Business College, soon to be joined by many more.

Dr. Peirce leased Handel and Haydn Hall from the Hand in Hand insurance company. The "pumper" (below, left) was part of the fire fighting equipment housed by the company on the ground floor of the Harrison Building in 1865. The advertisement (below) appeared on the reverse of a stereopticon photograph of the interior of Handel and Haydn Hall.

A copy of the original business ledger of the Union Business College (pictured below) is opened to reveal the school's first registrants.

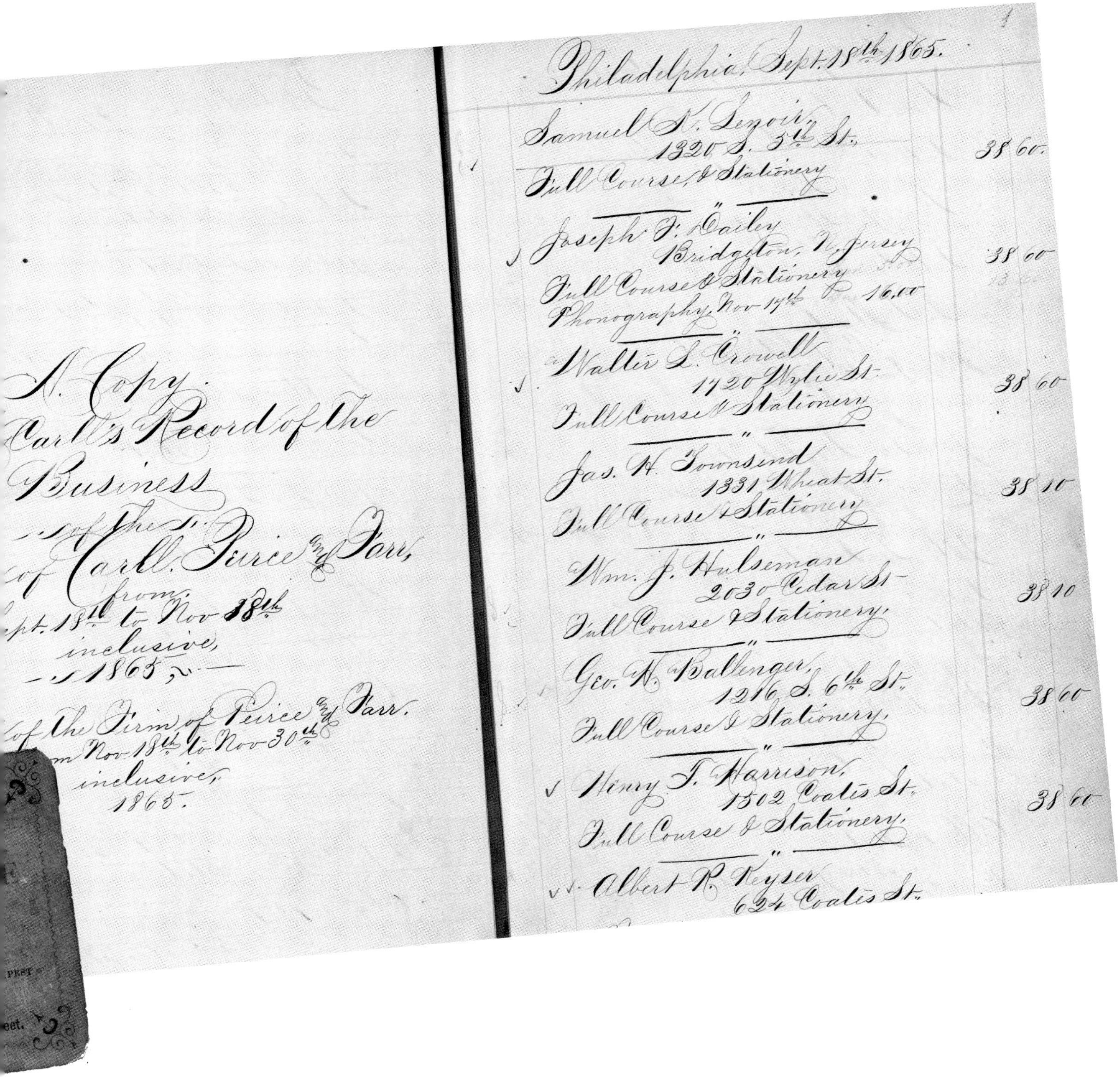

A. Copy
Carll's Record of the
Business
of the
Carll. Peirce & Parr,
from
Sept. 18th to Nov 18th
inclusive,
1865.

of the Firm of Peirce & Parr.
from Nov. 18th to Nov 30th
inclusive,
1865.

Philadelphia, Sept. 18th 1865.

Samuel K. Lezoit, 1320 S. 5th St. Full Course, & Stationery	38 60.
Joseph F. Dailey, Bridgeton, N. Jersey. Full Course & Stationery. Phonography Nov 17th 16.00	38 60
Walter L. Crowell, 1720 Wylie St. Full Course & Stationery	38 60
Jas. H. Townsend, 1331 Wheat St. Full Course & Stationery	38 10
Wm. J. Hulseman, 2030 Cedar St. Full Course & Stationery.	38 10
Geo. H. Ballenger, 1216 S. 6th St. Full Course & Stationery.	38 60
Henry T. Harrison, 1502 Coates St. Full Course & Stationery.	38 60
Albert R. Keyser, 624 Coates St.	

The Peirce Philosophy of Business Education

Although Europe had embraced the concept of industrial or vocational education, largely as a state-sponsored movement, the American academic community resisted this change. While many American commercial schools were excellent, other less scrupulous schools had also arisen, often combining wildly impossible guarantees of employment with unqualified instruction to taint the reputation of business education in general.

The business schools' insistence on terming themselves "colleges" added to the confusion. Then, as in modern America, the term "college" or "university" carried an understood imprimatur of advanced academic achievement. In an era before standards of accreditation and state licensing had been formally introduced in education, however, the terms lacked legal definition, and therefore were unrestricted in usage. Colleges and universities held a virtual monopoly in education beyond the high school, and the new business schools hoped to break that monopoly. Although the content of their curriculum did not conform to the academic model in operation at the time, business and other vocational schools adopted this term in an effort to gain credibility as an alternative to classical higher education.

Academics, steeped in the traditions of classical education, were quick to denounce the methods and value of their new competitors. Charges of charlatanism and quackery stung even the responsible commercial schools. This climate of doubt worried Peirce and his partners in the Union Business College, and they worked hard to establish an aura of respectability for their school.

In 1866, tuition for the full course was raised to $60, not including the cost of books and supplies.

A few quotations from the early literature of the college convey the tone of propriety, honesty, and practical good sense which characterized the approach of Peirce and his partners.

"A misunderstanding of the design and a prejudice against the management of Commercial Colleges has long existed. This arises primarily from the depreciation of the utility of the instruction imparted, and a distrust of the rash promises and specious advantages advertised by some institutions....We claim no fictitious advantages, and make no specious promises, but point, with confidence to the fact that [in 1866] over five hundred of our pupils are now enjoying the benefits of the knowledge acquired at our Institution."

"We are convinced that the present system of Commercial Colleges is capable of decided improvement. A long experience in different institutions has enabled us to separate the solid and the beneficial features from the showy and prejudicial pretensions."

"The demand for the merely learned is decreasing. That for the practical and useful is increasing; and the practical and useful are demanded alone, detached from everything else."

"We have no desire to assume for this Institution any higher rank than that of a plain, substantial and efficient school for the education of business men....it is free from all branches foreign to this design and all novelties introduced for effect."

"It is no longer necessary to waste the most active, ambitious and energetic years of life behind the desk, acquiring slowly, often imperfectly, a knowledge of one particular business, with a total ignorance of the general principles which govern all others."

C. B. Allaire (right) was one of the first UBC students in 1865. He graduated February 9, 1866, and his is the first name to be recorded in the book of graduates.

The Curriculum of Union Business College

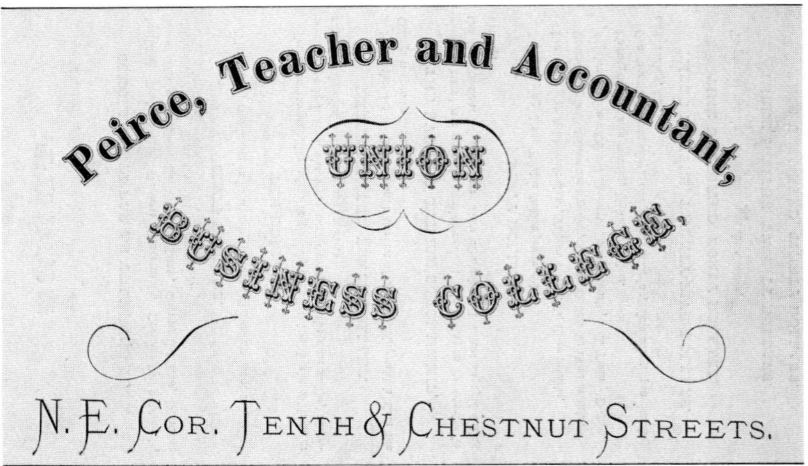

Dr. Peirce based the educational foundations of the Union Business College on quality, practicality, and convenience. The partners designed the school to fill a specific vocational niche, business education. Dr. Peirce had no intention of providing study of science, literature, or other elements of a classical university education. He did not dispute the value of liberal education, but recognized that in terms of time and money, it was out of the reach of most.

Not even an expensive and time-consuming college education would prepare one for a career in business. In 1865, no American university offered a business program. Business skills—book-keeping, accounting, retailing, banking—were customarily learned informally through work experience. Peirce was convinced that American industrial and commercial activity would mushroom in the post–Civil War decades, and that the demand for competent clerical workers and other business professionals would rise with it. Given these circumstances, Peirce believed that a school, offering a cogent, formalized education in business procedures with a minimal investment of time and money would have broad appeal within practically all classes of the American work force.

The concept of industrial, or vocational education, which would gain momentum in the United States throughout the late 19th century, was still a relative novelty at the time of the founding of Union Business College. The first commercial "colleges" appeared in the United States in the 1840s, but only a few, notable among these the Bryant and Stratton chain in the mid-West, enjoyed much long-lasting success. Even in 1870, the report of the United States Commissioner of Education in a single, short paragraph on commercial education, noted only twenty-six commercial schools operating in the United States, with a total student body of less than 6000.

Early catalogs and brochures clearly spelled out the scope of the Union Business College education.

THE UNION

Business College,

OF PHILADELPHIA.

Organized by an Association of Gentlemen of Liberal Education and Long Experience in the Business,

TO FURNISH ALL CLASSES OF SOCIETY

A PRACTICAL BUSINESS EDUCATION.

ORGANIZATION.

The Institution is organized upon a permanent and substantial basis as a first-class Business College. The studies included in the Course are such as furnish the necessary knowledge and qualifications of a business man. It is divided into four Departments, under the direction of the actual proprietors, who are directly interested in its success.

The Commercial Department is under the control of Thomas May Peirce, A.M., whose qualifications are the result of actual experience in business, and nearly seven years' earnest teaching. Those who are acquainted, however slightly, with the past few years' history of the public schools of Norristown or Philadelphia, know with what success he has taught, and what may be expected of the Commercial Department of The Union Business College in his hands.

The Penmanship is in charge of Mr. C. N. Farr, Jr., who has been connected with Commercial Colleges in the capacity of

---

Union Business College,

HANDEL AND HAYDN HALL,

Eighth and Spring Garden Sts.,

PHILADELPHIA.

THOMAS MAY PEIRCE, A.M.,

President and Consulting Accountant.

EXTRAORDINARY INDUCEMENTS!

NOVEL & PERMANENT ARRANGEMENT OF BUSINESS COLLEGE TERMS,

From April 1 to October 1, 1866,

AND SUCCEEDING YEARS.

LIFE SCHOLARSHIPS, including Bookkeeping, Business Correspondence, Forms and Customs, Commercial Arithmetic, Business Penmanship, Detecting Counterfeit Money, and Commercial Law.

TWENTY-FIVE DOLLARS.

SCHOLARSHIPS, including the same Subjects as above

Time Limited to Three Months.

TWENTY DOLLARS.

Penmanship, Three Months, ... $7

Penmanship and Arithmetic, Three Months, . . $10

The saving of coal and gas in the summer months is an advantage of such importance as enables the management of this College to make a considerable reduction in the summer rates.

From October 1, 1866, to April 1, 1867,

And succeeding years, as before.

Life Scholarships, ... $35

Scholarships, 3 months, ... $25

Penmanship, 3 months, ... $10

Penmanship and Arithmetic, 3 months, ... $12

Special Terms for Clubs, Soldiers, and for the Sons of Ministers and Teachers.

DAY AND EVENING INSTRUCTION FOR BOTH SEXES AND ALL AGES,

In Banking, Storekeeping, Bookkeeping, Penmanship, Pen Drawing, Photography, Arithmetic, Mensuration, Algebra, Geometry, Analytical Geometry, The Calculus, Navigation, Surveying, Engineering, Gauging, Mining, Mechanical Drawing, Commercial Law, German, Telegraphing, and the English Branches, at moderate prices.

Endorsed by the public as the most successful Business College of the country, as is evidenced by the fact, that

FOUR HUNDRED AND TWO STUDENTS

have entered in the

First Six Months of its Existence.

Principals of Departments:

THOMAS MAY PEIRCE, A.M.,

GEORGE B. SNYDER, R. S. BARNES,

C. N. FARR, Jr., J. T. REYNOLDS,

HENRY KEIM, A. E. ROGERSON, A.M., C.E.

THE UNION BUSINESS COLLEGE. 9

The Course of Instruction.

The educational department of the College is divided into three branches:—the Commercial Course, the Special Branches and the Teachers' Course.

THE COMMERCIAL COURSE

Includes every study necessary to form a perfect system of commercial education and every facility requisite to impart a practical business training, by a system combining theory and practice in a series of actual business transactions. The studies are

Bookkkeeping,
SINGLE AND DOUBLE ENTRY,
Penmanship,
Commercial Arithmetic,
Letter Writing,
Business Customs and Forms,
Commercial Law,
Detecting Counterfeit Money,
Declamation and Orthography.

In addition, LECTURES are delivered from time to time upon various subjects connected with the studies enumerated. A scholarship for the full course entitles the holder to attendance upon these; and as the time is unlimited, he will be privileged to proceed as rapidly or as leisurely as convenient, and to review without extra expense.

Such additions as Declamation and Orthography have been added to accommodate those whose early advantages have been limited.

THE SPECIAL BRANCHES.

As our reasons for discarding a number of special branches have already been given, it is unnecessary to specify those which have led us to retain the following. They are:

Business Penmanship,
Commercial Arithmetic,
Ornamental Penmanship.

THE

COURSE OF INSTRUCTION OF THE

Union Business College,

N. E. COR. TENTH & CHESTNUT STS,

(Second Floor,)

CONTAINS IN ADDITION TO

BOOK-KEEPING,

Penmanship & Arithmetic,

(The usual Studies of a Business course.)

ELOCUTION, by Prof. Philip Lawrence.
DETECTING COUNTERFEIT MONEY, by Prof. Jas. A. Pettet.
COMMERCIAL LAW, by J. T. Pratt, Esq. of the Philad'a Bar.
LETTER WRITING, by Prof. J. H. Warren.
ORTHOGRAPHY in an original manner, by the Principal.

Each Gentleman an expert in his profession.

THESE

EXTRA STUDIES

ARE TAUGHT

Without Extra Charge.

M'Calla & Stavely, Prs., 237-9 Dock St., Phila.

After a period of early experimentation, the Union Business College curriculum settled in, and experienced remarkably few major changes over the following decades. Its established programs proved successful, and there was little reason to enact major changes. Peirce himself was explicit as to the skills he thought were important in business. "As we conceive it, a good business education is a correct and scientific knowledge of accounts, expertness in the calculations of commercial arithmetic, a rapid, legible and handsome handwriting, the ability to compose a business letter, a knowledge of business forms and customs, and an acquaintance with the details of business transactions....It includes further an insight into Commercial Law, an understanding of the general principles of trade and commerce, and an appreciation of the duties and responsibilities of a merchant."

He thought the effort of some business schools to give emphasis to the areas usually thought of as the Liberal Arts was to diminish and dilute the core of basic skills more appropriate to business. "To extend the range into the sciences, the classics and the higher mathematics, is to weaken the efforts, divert the attention and retard the progress of the teacher and the student."

His teaching methods as well as his curriculum content gave emphasis to the practical, hands-on approach. "The system [of teaching employed at the Union Business College] is based upon the idea that the senses are better conveyencers of knowledge than the imagination." It is "a rare and effective combination of theory and practice." He spelled out parallels to other types of education. "What the model school is to the normal [teachers'] school or the hospital to the medical school, the actual business department is to the business school."

Through the actual Business Department, "the College becomes a theatre of actual business operations."

"The rawness and crudeness which a student who has just finished a course of bookkeeping exhibits to a business man, evoking his condemnation of school bookkeeping and his emphatic condemnation of countinghouse bookkeeping, is here removed from the student by the friction of business as real as that in any jobbing or commission house in the city. Personally, I regard the development of this banking and business department as the most valuable single item in a commercial course."

Thomas May Peirce, 1893

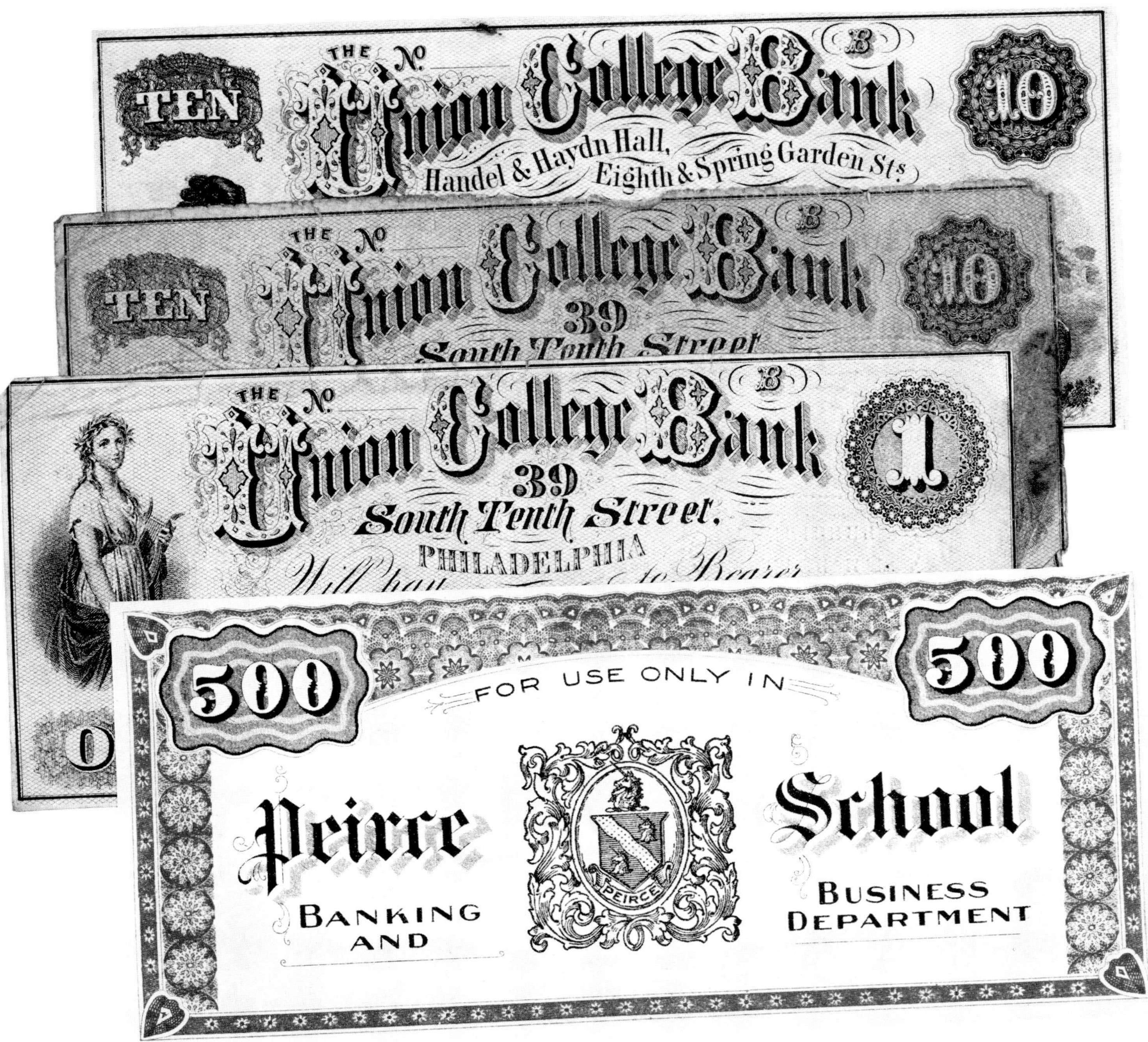

Students in the Actual Business Department conducted transactions with currency issued by the school bank.

During the late 1860s, Thomas May Peirce published a trade journal, Peirce's Practical Educator. The October, 1868 issue included an editorial by Thomas May Peirce, regarding the uneven reputation of business education: "Like every other innovation, the business schools are meeting with strenuous opposition through ignorance and prejudice."

PEIRCE'S PRACTICA

POPULAR INSTRUCTI

UNION BUSINESS COLLEG

HARRISON BUILDING,

Occupying the Whole Square on Eighth Street from Spring Garden to Green Street,

THE POPULAR HANDEL & HAYDN HALL USED AS A COLLEGE RO

OFFICE OF COLLEGE, No. 531 N. EIGHTH ST.

Entrance for Gentlemen, No. 533 N. Eighth street. Entrance for Ladies, No. 734 Green st

No educational institution of the land is possessed of rooms so large, well ventilated, or ligh furnished with better appointments.

A large and talented corps of Teachers. Faithful, intelligent teaching of students, its claim to p favor.

TWO HUNDRED AND SEVENTY PUPILS IN DAILY ATTENDANCE, PER ROLL B

A fact which implies public confidence in its soundness, as well as declares most emphatically its suc

The pioneer in placing Business Colleges among the strictly educational institutions of the l discarding from the beginning the tinsel and trappings which excite the disgust of the business com and retard the progressive educational tendencies of the age.

The fundamental ideas of managing an educational institution recognized, and a sound wholesom pline inaugurated and maintained.

A good handwriting the proper foundation of a business education, a cardinal principle of its m ment.

For extent and elegance of rooms, appropriateness of location, intellectual strength and energy of t soundness of discipline, practicability of course of instruction, and success of its students in p secured for them by the College Management, it maintains that pre-eminence which an enlighten scientious and faithful management of business secures over fogyism or charlatanry.

His "actual business department," involved a set of business transactions, such as interviews, purchasing and selling exchanges, supervisory situations and other experiences that a modern generation would describe as "role playing." Dr. Peirce constructed an entire business community in miniature on campus, maintaining a retailing/wholesaling firm, bank, insurance company, and post office. Students went into business for themselves, paying rent and utility bills, and making transactions among themselves that were faithful in every detail to a real-world business experience.

Some other business schools maintained similar arrangements. What was unique about Peirce's approach was that he insisted that students be thrust into a real business environment, not knowing what would occur next, rather than follow text book exercises. In this regard, his effort to establish role-playing situations anticipated some of psychological theories popular in education more than a century later. Through the "actual business department," Peirce said, "the College becomes a theatre of actual business operations." The vast experience of the teachers of Union Business College, Peirce claimed, enabled them to develop their "own system of teaching" that was more efficient and effective than others'.

Course work in the early business curriculum involved the study of Bookkeeping, Penmanship, Commercial Law, Business Correspondence and Forms, and Commercial Arithmetic. Peirce also provided regular lectures on Commercial Law, Ethics, and Commerce and Trade.

JCATOR, OCTOBER, 1868. 3

AT POPULAR PRICES.

FACULTY.

OFFICERS:

THOMAS MAY PEIRCE, A.M., *President, Consulting Accountant and Conductor of Col'eje Examinations.*

MAJOR A. J. NEWBY, *Secretary.*

H. BUCKMINSTER, *Assistant Secretary and Office Superintendent.*

CHESTER N. FARR, Jr., *Ornamental Penman.*

TEACHERS:

IOMAS MAY PEIRCE, A.M., Principal of the Actual Business Department and Teacher of Book-keeping, Business Forms and Customs, Mathematics, Commercial Law and Philology.

AJOR A. J. NEWBY, Principal of Theoretical Department and Teacher of Business Writing, Flourishing, Book-keeping, Arithmetic, Business Forms and Letter-Writing.

AVID A. PRICE, Teacher of Book-keeping, Business Forms and Arithmetic.

HN N. PRICE, Superintendent of Union College Bank, Thomas M. Peirce & Co.'s Importing and Jobbing House, Union College Express Co., Union College Insurance Co., and Conveyancer's Office, and Teacher of Book-keeping and Business Customs and Forms.

OFESSOR JAMES A. PETTET, Teacher on Genuine, Counterfeit and Altered Government and National Bank Notes and Small Currency.

S. IRENE C. WHITE BRADLEY, Teacher of Elocution.

ll the above Studies are taught by the respective Teachers announced, without any **EXTRA IARGE** to the Pupils.

The most talented and best-paid Corps of Teachers to be found in any Business College of the United tes.

The advantage of a thorough knowledge of currency patent to the business community.

The advertisement (at left) appeared in the October, 1868 issue of Peirce's Practical Educator. Below: the publication's flag.

In addition, the college in 1865 offered specialized courses in "the special branches," including Engineering and Surveying, Higher Mathematics, Algebra, Geometry, Trigonometry, Ornamental Penmanship, and Phonography. Courses in "declamation" and "orthography" were added to the curriculum, as well as a "special normal course" for the training of public school teachers in 1866.

Top left: E. T. Stotesbury, graduate of the first class. Above: Third floor classroom, Harrison Building. Below: A diploma from the 1860s. Facing page: A "Life Scholarship" which entitled a student to instruction for an unlimited time. Far right: Frank Thompson, a classmate of Stotesbury.

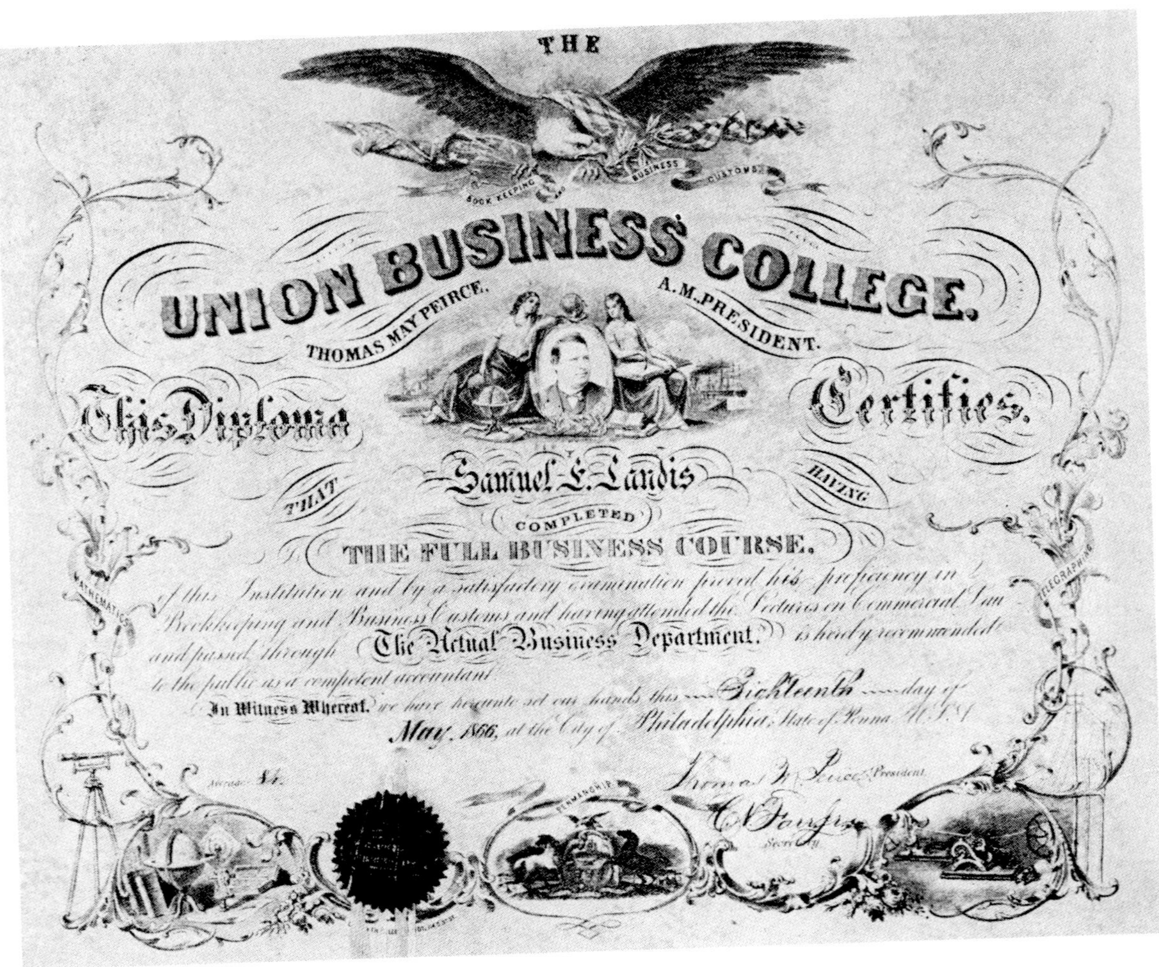

THE

BOOK KEEPING AND BUSINESS CUSTOMS

UNION BUSINESS COLLEGE.

THOMAS MAY PEIRCE, A.M. PRESIDENT.

This Diploma Certifies.

THAT Samuel E. Landis HAVING COMPLETED THE FULL BUSINESS COURSE, of this Institution and by a satisfactory examination proved his proficiency in Bookkeeping and Business Customs and having attended the Lectures on Commercial Law and passed through The Actual Business Department, is hereby recommended to the public as a competent accountant.

In Witness Whereof, we have hereunto set our hands this Eighteenth day of May, 1866, at the City of Philadelphia, State of Penna. U.S.A.

Thomas M. Peirce President.

Secretary.

MATHEMATICS

TELEGRAPHING

PENMANSHIP

YOUTH IS THE BANKER OF OLD AGE

Scholarship of the Union Business College of Philadelphia

No.

SCHOLARSHIP

This Certifies that for and in consideration of the sum of Thirty Five Dollars the receipt whereof is hereby acknowledged Mr James Lewisson has become a Student in this Institution subject to the rules and regulations of the Institution entitled to all the privileges of said institution and to Instruction for an unlimited time, in Bookkeeping, Commercial Calculation, Business Penmanship Correspondence and Forms and to an attendance upon the Lectures.

In Testimony whereof we have hereto set our hand this 9th day of April in the Year 1866

Thomas M. Peirce

Business Superintendent

NOT TRANSFERABLE

The school's early curriculum included a department devoted to general studies. The name of this department varied from catalog to catalog and year to year, variously entitled "English," "Teacher's," "Academic," and "Preparatory" department. This department covered the basics of English and Arithmetic that could be used to secure an elementary school teaching position. This department, which featured a great deal of personal instruction, was also used for secondary level work for those whose background did not sufficiently prepare them to begin their business or shorthand studies.

To accommodate fully employed students, Union Business College utilized a practice, pioneered by established business schools such as Bryant and Stratton before the Civil War, which allowed a great deal of flexibility in class attendance. Students could enter at any time, and the time for completing any course of study was unlimited. Evening sessions were open from the first. The Union Business College "Life Scholarship" enabled the student to attend as many or as few of the classes and special lectures as he or she wished. Students could enter any day of the year, and having paid tuition, could "consult their own convenience and interests in their attendance," devoting "as many of the specified business hours as they please." The time required for completion of the courses was varied, depending on "the application and previous qualification of the student." The average time mentioned in the first catalog was 10–12 weeks, but the proprietors noted that the course had been completed in as little as 28 working days, and as long as 13 months.

Unlike other schools of the day, the Union Business College held classes year round. In typically forthright manner, an early catalog explained the simple rationale for this practice: "Business Colleges are managed as Business Houses and hence, remain open all summer."

Growth and Early Success

By the end of the first day of classes, Union Business College had enrolled 31 students. Of these, all but two pursued the full business course; one took the penmanship course, and one combined arithmetic and penmanship. In the school's first month, a total of 195 students enrolled, most from Philadelphia, but some from such "distant" locales as Pottsville, Pennsylvania, Camden and Trenton, New Jersey, Lombardville, Maryland, Rockland, Maine, and Aurora, Illinois. Students in the full course paid tuition of $35, $5 less if paid in full in one month's time. By the end of the first year, a total of 569 students, including 68 women, had attended Union Business College.

In 1866, Union Business College published its first textbook, the Union Business College Guide. This handbook to the theoretical and practical exercises of the business department was the forerunner to the widely-used Peirce Manual of Bookkeeping, and the first of many textbooks to be authored and published by the school over the following eighty-five years.

Early catalogs reflected a ongoing experimentation with the curriculum. Programs such as the Teachers' Course—teaching "the English branches generally taught in public and private schools," which included Grammar, Elocution, Natural Philosophy, Geometry, Algebra, Mensuration, and Arithmetic—underwent almost constant revision. As finally conceived, the Teachers' Department served as a basic skills course in secondary level work, "for those whose early education has been neglected," or who could not "without further work" qualify for the Commercial Course.

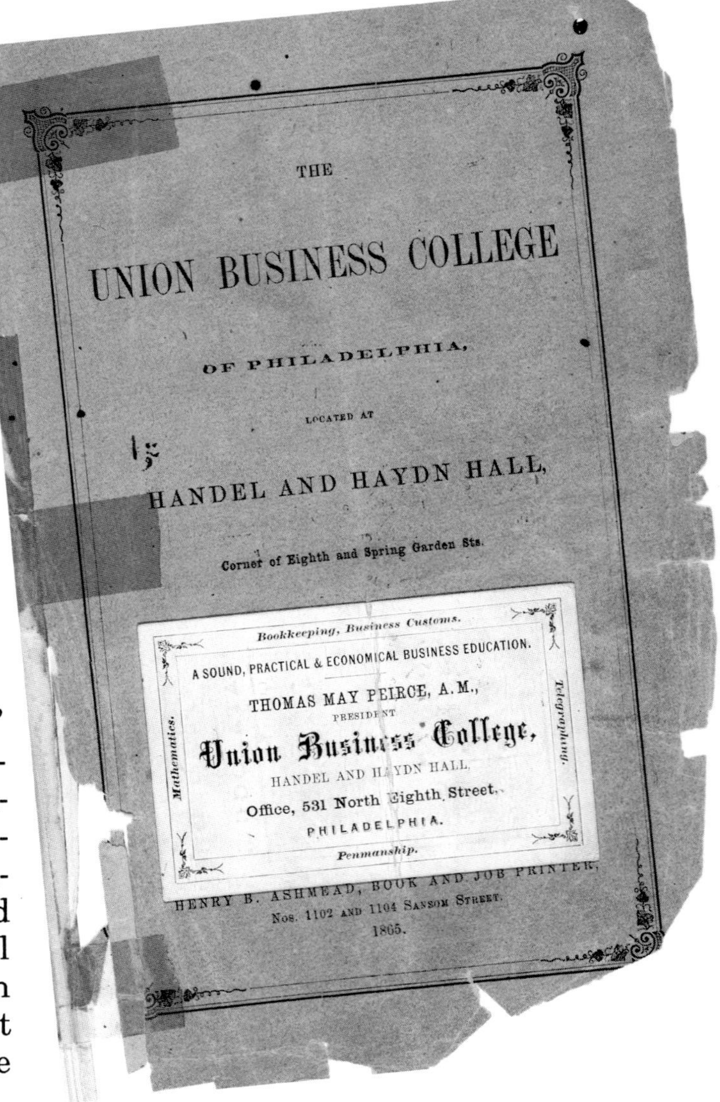

THE

UNION BUSINESS COLLEGE

OF PHILADELPHIA,

LOCATED AT

HANDEL AND HAYDN HALL,

Corner of Eighth and Spring Garden Sts.

Bookkeeping, Business Customs.

A SOUND, PRACTICAL & ECONOMICAL BUSINESS EDUCATION.

THOMAS MAY PEIRCE, A.M.,

PRESIDENT

Union Business College,

HANDEL AND HAYDN HALL.

Office, 531 North Eighth Street.

PHILADELPHIA.

Mathematics. Telegraphing. Penmanship.

HENRY B. ASHMEAD, BOOK AND JOB PRINTER,

Nos. 1102 and 1104 Sansom Street.

1865.

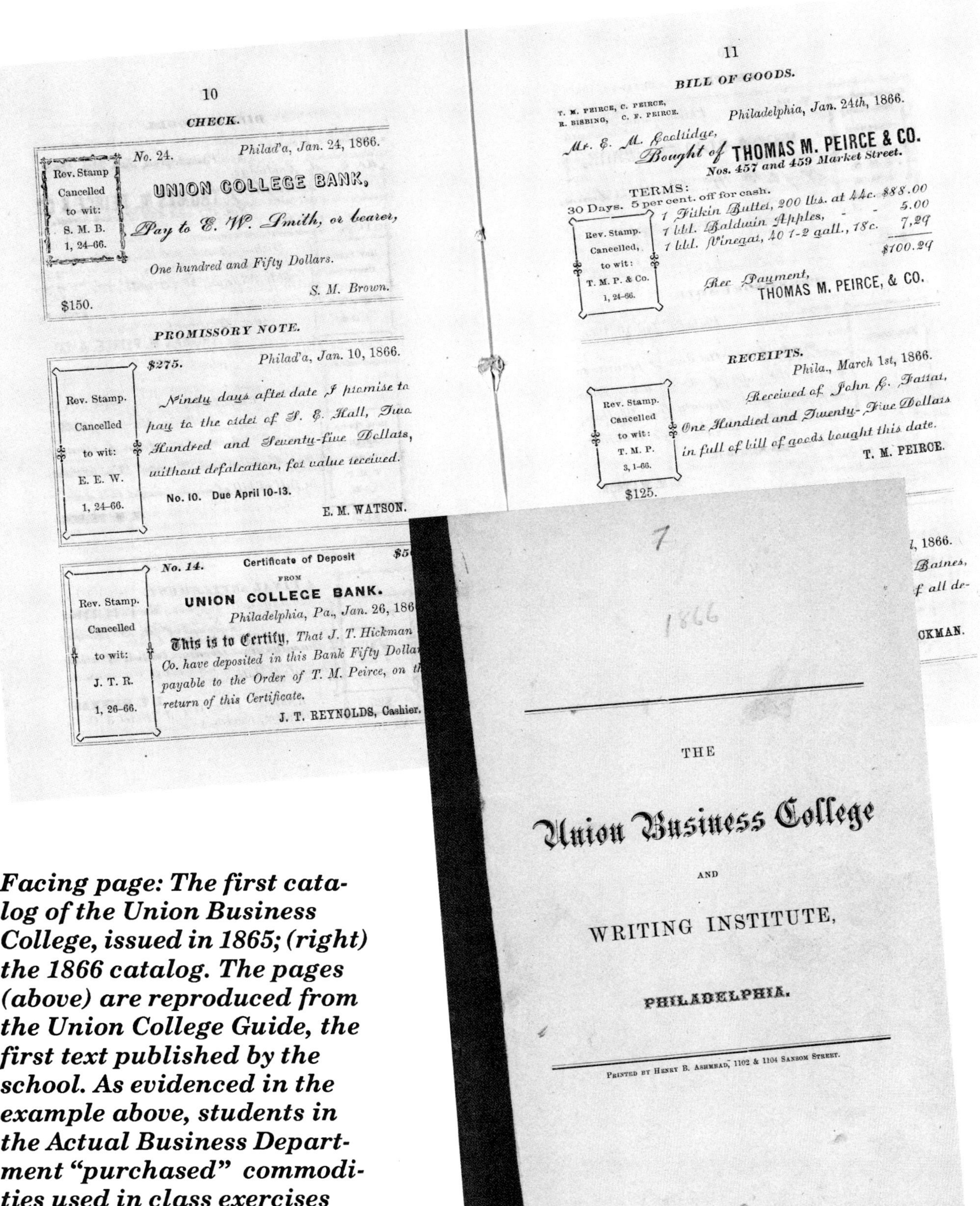

10

CHECK.

No. 24. *Philad'a, Jan. 24, 1866.*

Rev. Stamp Cancelled to wit: S. M. B. 1, 24-66.

UNION COLLEGE BANK,

Pay to E. W. Smith, or bearer,

One hundred and Fifty Dollars.

S. M. Brown.

$150.

PROMISSORY NOTE.

$275. *Philad'a, Jan. 10, 1866.*

Rev. Stamp. Cancelled to wit: E. E. W. 1, 24-66.

Ninety days after date I promise to pay to the order of S. E. Hall, Two Hundred and Seventy-five Dollars, without defalcation, for value received.

No. 10. Due April 10-13.

E. M. WATSON.

No. 14. Certificate of Deposit $5

FROM

UNION COLLEGE BANK.

Philadelphia, Pa., Jan. 26, 186

Rev. Stamp. Cancelled to wit: J. T. R. 1, 26-66.

This is to Certify, *That J. T. Hickman Co. have deposited in this Bank Fifty Dolla payable to the Order of T. M. Peirce, on th return of this Certificate.*

J. T. REYNOLDS, Cashier.

11

BILL OF GOODS.

T. M. PEIRCE, C. PEIRCE, R. BISBING, C. F. PEIRCE.

Philadelphia, Jan. 24th, 1866.

Mr. E. M. Coolidge,

Bought of THOMAS M. PEIRCE & CO.

Nos. 457 and 459 Market Street.

TERMS:

30 Days. 5 per cent. off for cash.

Rev. Stamp. Cancelled, to wit: T. M. P. & Co. 1, 24-66.

1 Firkin Butter, 200 lbs. at 44c.	*$88.00*
1 bbl. Baldwin Apples, - -	*5.00*
1 bbl. Vinegar, 40 1-2 gall., 18c.	*7,29*
	$100.29

Rec. Payment,

THOMAS M. PEIRCE, & CO.

RECEIPTS.

Phila., March 1st, 1866.

Rev. Stamp. Cancelled to wit: T. M. P. 3, 1-66.

Received of John G. Farrar, One Hundred and Twenty-Five Dollars in full of bill of goods bought this date.

T. M. PEIRCE.

$125.

l, 1866.

Baines,

f all de-

CKMAN.

7

1866

THE

Union Business College

AND

WRITING INSTITUTE,

PHILADELPHIA.

PRINTED BY HENRY B. ASHMEAD, 1102 & 1104 SANSOM STREET.

Facing page: The first catalog of the Union Business College, issued in 1865; (right) the 1866 catalog. The pages (above) are reproduced from the Union College Guide, the first text published by the school. As evidenced in the example above, students in the Actual Business Department "purchased" commodities used in class exercises from a school wholesaling firm, Thomas M. Peirce and Company.

A "Ladies Department" and the Ladies' Institute of Art operated at the early Union Business College under the direction of Miss A. A. Chapman, Principal. These departments incorporated several courses which varied from the strictly practical approach characteristic of most of the curriculum. An early listing of Miss Chapman's offerings included work in fine arts, music, and French.

Dr. Peirce, however, was careful to emphasize the school's specialization in business-related disciplines. Speaking of the Teacher's Course, he noted, "It will be remarked that this department is entirely distinct from the Commercial Department. The principle energies of the College are directed to imparting a sound, practical and comprehensive business education." After this has been accomplished, "the superfluous energies of the College are then diverted to other of the more practical ends in the educational department."

Peirce scheduled periodic examinations, which would determine whether or not the student should proceed to another level. "Throughout the course the student is subjected to a rigid examination, and his progress depends upon his thor-

"The door of Peirce College has been opened for women and it remains open and it will never be shut again."

Thomas May Peirce, 1893

Facing page: This illustration from the first catalog apparently depicts a third floor room in the Harrison building. Rooms on this floor, above the main classroom, were used for the Ladies' Department and for private instruction. Below: a "Manual for Student Traders" published about 1885.

ough understanding of what has been taught him before. The final examination is conducted with the same thoroughness and rigidity as have marked the examinations of the President as a Grammar School Principal." Examinations were held each Friday for students who felt ready to graduate.

After the first year, Peirce noted that over 500 of the 550 pupils found "confidential and lucrative positions as bookkeepers, salesmen, clerks, bank officers, teachers, and assistants. Consequently, the College discarded many of the "special branches" in order to concentrate on the essentials—bookkeeping, penmanship, and arithmetic. Peirce particularly credited the actual business department for the success in placing graduates, and he maintained that unique feature of the school through the other changes.

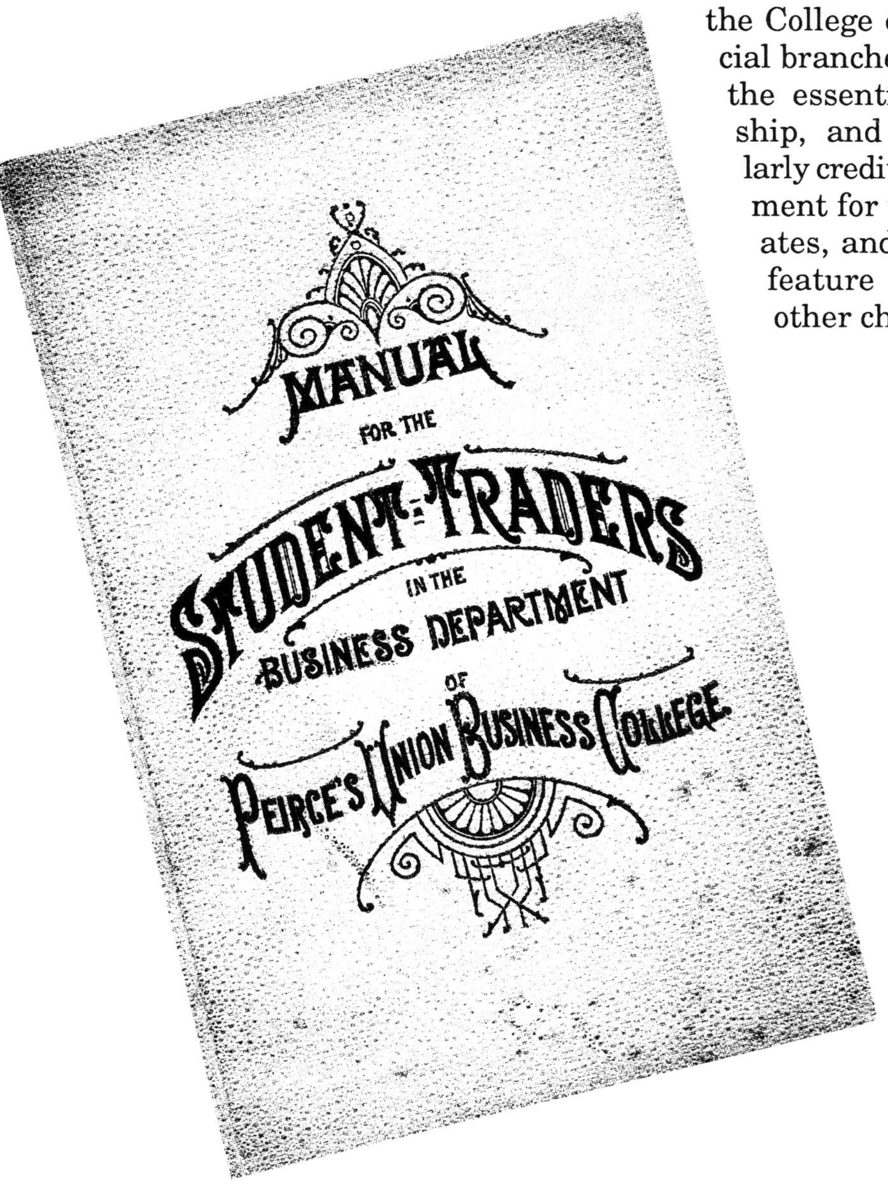

ESTABLISHED 1865.

PEIRCE'S

UNION BUSINESS COLLEGE,

No. 39 South Tenth Street,

PHILADELPHIA, PA.

CIRCULAR FOR THE TWELFTH COLLEGIATE YEAR,

Beginning September, 1876.

PHILADELPHIA:
THOMAS MAY PEIRCE.
1876.

Chapter 2
Peirce College of Business

With Handel and Haydn Hall really unsuited to formalized class work, especially under the Union Business College's "personal progress" system, Thomas May Peirce soon began looking for alternate quarters. In April, 1869 the school moved to the Inman Building at Tenth and Chestnut Streets, where it occupied the entire second floor. The addition of four new instructors doubled the size of the faculty to eight. The Teachers' Department was renamed the Department of English, and devoted entirely to preparatory and secondary-level work and general study. The new building also allowed room for the establishment of a library.

The Inman Building was to be only a temporary home for the Union Business College, but this location became the source of many pleasant recollections for former students in later years. One such fond memory involved the tasty delicacies available at Finelli's lunch room, on the first floor, during the noon hour. Few, including Principal Peirce, could ignore the tantalizing aroma of Signor Finelli's specialty, Italian fried oysters, that filled classrooms on the floor above as the lunch hour approached. The sight of John R. Harrison, the school janitor, scurrying toward the principal's office with a steaming tray from Finelli's was a frequently remarked-upon lunchtime ritual during these years.

The 1876 catalog (facing page) boasted the address of the Inman Building, 39 South Tenth Street, where the school had moved seven years earlier.

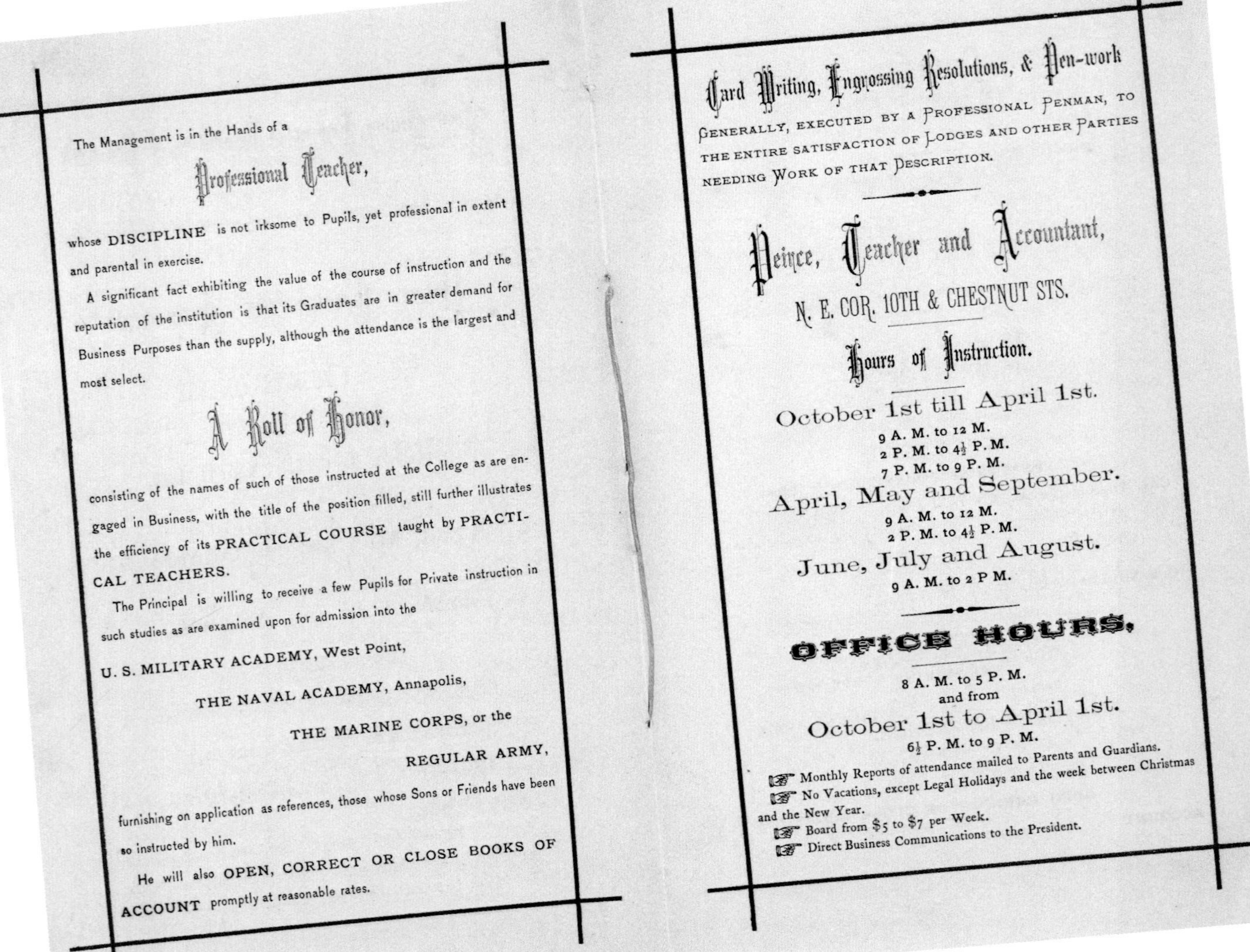

The Management is in the Hands of a

Professional Teacher,

whose **DISCIPLINE** is not irksome to Pupils, yet professional in extent and parental in exercise.

A significant fact exhibiting the value of the course of instruction and the reputation of the institution is that its Graduates are in greater demand for Business Purposes than the supply, although the attendance is the largest and most select.

A Roll of Honor,

consisting of the names of such of those instructed at the College as are engaged in Business, with the title of the position filled, still further illustrates the efficiency of its **PRACTICAL COURSE** taught by **PRACTICAL TEACHERS.**

The Principal is willing to receive a few Pupils for Private instruction in such studies as are examined upon for admission into the

U. S. MILITARY ACADEMY, West Point,

THE NAVAL ACADEMY, Annapolis,

THE MARINE CORPS, or the

REGULAR ARMY,

furnishing on application as references, those whose Sons or Friends have been so instructed by him.

He will also **OPEN, CORRECT OR CLOSE BOOKS OF ACCOUNT** promptly at reasonable rates.

Card Writing, Engrossing Resolutions, & Pen-work

GENERALLY, EXECUTED BY A PROFESSIONAL PENMAN, TO THE ENTIRE SATISFACTION OF LODGES AND OTHER PARTIES NEEDING WORK OF THAT DESCRIPTION.

Peirce, Teacher and Accountant,

N. E. COR. 10TH & CHESTNUT STS.

Hours of Instruction.

October 1st till April 1st.

9 A. M. to 12 M.
2 P. M. to 4½ P. M.
7 P. M. to 9 P. M.

April, May and September.

9 A. M. to 12 M.
2 P. M. to 4½ P. M.

June, July and August.

9 A. M. to 2 P M.

OFFICE HOURS,

8 A. M. to 5 P. M.
and from
October 1st to April 1st.
6½ P. M. to 9 P. M.

☞ Monthly Reports of attendance mailed to Parents and Guardians.
☞ No Vacations, except Legal Holidays and the week between Christmas and the New Year.
☞ Board from $5 to $7 per Week.
☞ Direct Business Communications to the President.

By 1870 the original partnership and working arrangement with Farr and the Carlls was completely dissolved. With the success of the commercial course, Peirce abandoned the Special Branches, including the Ladies Institute of Art to concentrate on the basics of a sound business education. Dr. Peirce hired the Reverend John Thompson as Business Manager to enable Peirce to devote more time to teaching and his increasingly strenuous outside pursuits by relieving him of administrative trivia.

Dr. Peirce increased the pace of his outside activities in the 1870s. The leaflet (pictured above) solicits private clients as well as Union Business College students. Facing page: Reverend John Thompson.

Although enrollment frequently topped 900 during these years, Principal Peirce earned the respect of students through his accessibility and his sincere interest in their personal progress and welfare. According to well-established legend, despite the large number of students, Dr. Peirce addressed each of them by name.

At the Inman Building, the Union Business College was able to assume a greater degree of structure and formality in its presentation of classes. The Commercial Course now met from 9 to 2 each day. Classes in the "Academical" Department (as the English Department became called) were held from 2 to 5 daily. Night school was in session three days per week from 7 to 9 P.M. Almost apologetically, Dr. Peirce announced an end to the flexible self-scheduling of the past, assuming a more "Disciplinary Management, Not irksome to the pupil, yet professional in extent, and parental in exercise." Students might still enter at any time of year, however, and progress at their own pace, but were required to be present during school hours. Attendance was monitored by roll call three times per day.

The general education in the Academical Department was available to anyone, as a preparation to the work in the commercial course or otherwise. It was suggested that the instruction in this department was particularly well-suited to "Farmers and others who can spare their sons but for a winter's schooling, in which to finish their education."

THE 1870s

The steady flow of Civil War veterans which helped fuel the expansion of business education began to abate in the early 1870s, and the Union Business College ended its spectacular early cycle of growth. Many other schools, less well established than the Union Business College, were forced to close, and those that remained open struggled to maintain attendance levels. Union Business College attendance, although significantly below its peak of 900, remained relatively stable during this period, averaging roughly 500 annually.

Thomas May Peirce may have seen this lull as a welcome change from the hectic years of founding and growth. The slow pace in the 1870s enabled him to expand the range of his outside activities and fully explore other business and personal interests. As an expert accountant and accomplished penman, he once again, as he had before establishing the Union

Robert Whitaker

The above is a tracing of the name
Robert Whitaker as found at the end
of an alleged will dated May 7th 1878
now in the office of the Register of Wills
~~offic~~

A. I believe that the writing is simulated
and unnatural.

(a) The terminal part of the t in Robert,
thus, t shows a degree of constraint
inconsistent with the freedom shown in
the writing of Rober and the stem of the
t.

(b) The terminal part of the r in Whitaker
thus, r likewise shows a degree of constraint inconsistent with the freedom
shown in the writing of Whita.

(c) The whole of the last syllable of Whitaker, to wit,
Ker is made ~~and~~ in a constrained,
cramped hand, thus, ker, which is
at variance with the balance of the
writing, ~~save~~ excepting only the terminal
part of the t in Robert, before referred to.
Robert Whita (barring the terminal
part of the t) is written in a freer, easier
hand; Ker is written in a very cramped,
constrained hand. It is not natural
that one should use two hand-writings

Business College, offered his services on a consulting basis. In addition, Dr. Peirce advertised his willingness to "receive a few Pupils for Private instruction in such studies as are examined upon for admission into the U.S. Military Academy, West Point, The Naval Academy, Annapolis, The Marine Corps, or the Regular Army."

Peirce's outside businesses thrived. He rapidly became known as an expert in the lines of accountancy and penmanship. In the field of accounting, several of the texts which he authored were widely adopted in his own and other schools. In penmanship, his skill led to some intriguing assignments. He served several times as court expert in criminal cases involving fraud and forgery. In one of his more celebrated cases, Peirce was able to demonstrate tampering with the log book and lading manifests of a scuttled British ship. The captain of the ship claimed the right to a large insurance settlement for the loss of a valuable cargo of vanilla beans. The insurance company suspected fraud. On the basis of Peirce's testimony, an expedition was mounted to recover the ship, and its cargo, as Peirce had predicted, was discovered to be worthless ballast. Peirce gained a further measure of local celebrity in the Whitaker Will case, in which he proved the document of bequest to be a forgery.

1st Is the signature natural or simulated writing or simulated? Why?
2 - Is the signature Robert Whitaker to the will in the same hand writing as the sig. Robert Whitaker to the checks? Why?
3 - Is the signature Robert Whitaker to the will in the hand writing of any one whose writing is before you? Why?

Materials Relating to the Whitaker Will Case. Right: Dr. Peirce's own notes summarizing the questions put to him; (above right) tracings of the contested signature; (facing page) page one of Dr. Peirce's statement to the court.

Dr. Peirce also became active in civic and professional affairs. He was a trustee of Temple College and the Methodist Episcopal Hospital, president of the Bookkeepers' Benevolent Association of Philadelphia, and prominent in a number of church-related functions. Peirce also declined several lucrative and prestigious posts to remain at Peirce School, including the Consulship of the United States at Liverpool, and the Presidency of Girard College. In 1878, he served as Bank Assessor to the State of Pennsylvania. The following year, Peirce was elected president of the Business Educators' Association of America, and he received an honorary doctorate degree from Dickinson College.

Always interested in politics, as the 1870s drew to a close, Peirce became active in the Democratic Party. In 1880, he undertook an extensive speaking tour of Ohio, Indiana, and Maryland, stumping for Democratic presidential candidate Winfield S. Hancock. Despite Hancock's poor showing in the election, the success of this tour left Dr. Peirce seemingly poised on the verge of a political career, leading to his own candidacy for the post of Collector of Taxes later that year.

Peirce lost the election, and with it his hopes for a political career. However, his foray into public life possibly renewed his enthusiasm for teaching. The heightened perspective and increased personal stature that resulted from his experiences in the 1870s made him an even more effective educator, and, judging by the advances made by Union Business College in the next few years, he returned to the school with renewed purpose and vigor.

Facing page: Dr. Peirce's business card; (top right) a newspaper clipping announcing his candidacy for elected office.

> "... in general terms, we may pronounce education to be improving in proportion as it becomes utilitarian. It is improving in proportion as it renders men more fitted to avail themselves of the positions of agents in the production of wealth, and at the same time fits them to enjoy refined pleasure, and to seize upon all the opportunities for promoting their own or others' welfare, which are presented."
>
> Thomas May Peirce, 1878

THE NEW CANDIDATE FOR RECEIVER OF TAXES.

Professor Thomas May Peirce, last evening nominated by the Democratic Convention as their candidate for Receiver of Taxes, is the popular and efficient President of the Union Business College, at the northeast corner of Tenth and Chestnut streets, in this city. He has also an extensive practice as a consulting accountant. He is the son of Caleb Peirce, well known in Philadelphia as an advertising agent and manufacturer of printing ink. The Peirces belong to one of the oldest Quaker families in Pennsylvania, and the name is familiar in Philadelphia, Delaware, and Chester counties. George Peirce, one of the original settlers, is mentioned in the proprietary maps in lawyers' offices as the owner of a large tract of land, now Thornbury township, in Delaware county, which he named after his wife. Professor Peirce on the maternal side is the grandson of the Rev. Thomas P. May, deceased, who had charge of St. John's Episcopal Church at Moorestown; while his grand-uncle, the Rev. Dr. James May, was rector of St. Paul's Episcopal Church, on Third street below Walnut, in this city, and afterwards professor in the Divinity School at West Philadelphia. The new candidate for Receiver of Taxes has resided in the Thirteenth ward for the last eight years, and for ten years past has presided over the Union Business College and taught over five thousand pupils. He has always been identified with the Democratic organization, but has taken no active part since he attained his majority.

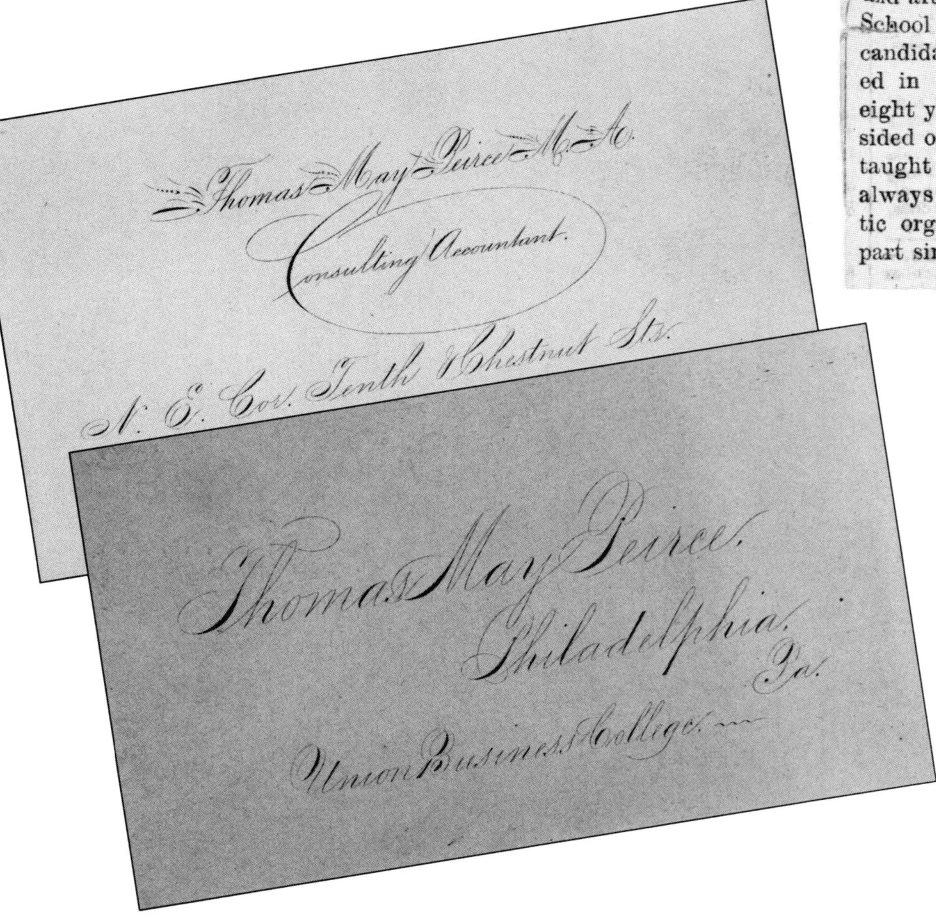

The Union Business College won national attention through its prize-winning exhibit at the Philadelphia Centennial in 1876. Clockwise from right: an exhibit specimen; obverse and reverse views of the gold medal awarded the school; and the statement of the judges.

THE CENTENNIAL DIPLOMA AND MEDAL

WAS AWARDED TO

Peirce's Union Business College,

Wednesday, September 27th, 1876.

DETAILS OF THE SAME:

The following named gentlemen were appointed by the United States Centennial Commission to act as Judges on Education and Science, at the International Exhibition, held in this city, from May 10th to November 10th, 1876:—

HON. ANDREW D. WHITE, LL. D.,
President of Cornell University,
ITHACA, N. Y.

D. C. GILMAN, LL. D.,
President of Johns Hopkins University,
BALTIMORE, MD.

HON. J. M. GREGORY, LL. D.,
President of the Illinois Industrial University,
CHAMPAIGN, ILL.

PROF. J. W. HOYT, LL. D.,
United States Commissioner to the Paris Exposition of 1867, and President Judge on Education and Science at the Vienna Exposition of 1873,
MADISON, WIS.

SIR CHARLES REED, M. P.,
Member of the London School Board,
LONDON, ENGLAND.

MR. RENÉ FOURET,
Of the firm of Hachette & Co., Publishers,
PARIS, FRANCE.

JUAN JOSÉ MARIN y LEON,
Colonel Royal Engineers, and Royal Commissioner from Spain to the Philadelphia International Exhibition,
MADRID, SPAIN.

PROF. DR. OTTO MARTIN TORELL,
Geologist,
SWEDEN.

After more than three months' careful examination of the various products submitted to them, they recommended PEIRCE'S UNION BUSINESS COLLEGE to the proper authorities for award. A brief description of the articles placed on exhibition by this institution, and examined by the above-named Judges, will be found on pages 20 and 21 of this Circular.

CERTIFIED COPY OF REPORT OF JUDGES.

The United States Centennial Commission announce the following Report as the basis of an award to PEIRCE'S UNION BUSINESS COLLEGE, Philadelphia, Penna., for Penmanship, Book-Keeping and Publications, and work showing courses of instruction:—

REPORT.

The exhibits afford evidence of excellent work in the different departments embraced, while the general plan and purposes of the institution also entitle it to commendation.

Besides the College proper, the institution embraces a well organized preparatory school, in order that none may have an excuse for ignorance of the ordinary English branches, proficiency in which should everywhere be considered a pre-requisite to admission to a commercial school.

A. T. GOSHORN, *Director-General.*
J. R. HAWLEY, *President.*

U.S.C.C. Seal. 1876.

ATTEST:
J. L. CAMPBELL, *Secretary.*

Thomas May Peirce's exhibitor's pass to the Centennial grounds.

Although the school had been successful in terms of numbers, in 1876 the Union Business College earned its first critical acclaim. Its exhibit at the Philadelphia Centennial Exhibition, held in Fairmount Park that year, received a gold medal in the category of commercial education. The College's winning exhibit consisted of seven parts: an elaborate penmanship exhibit; samples of school currency and commodities; descriptions of the mission of the school as well as its courses of instruction; text books in use at the school; and four large volumes containing samples of student work.

Edgar S. Trout, a graduate in 1874, was an excellent penman. He was selected to keep the books for the centennial corporation in 1876. The Centennial Memorial of Visitors, on which Trout recorded several thousand names, was deposited in the library of Congress following the centennial.

PEIRCE'S

UNION BUSINESS COLLEGE.

TELEGRAPHING,

Under the charge of

E. J. BENNETT,

Practical Operator.

In response to the demand so persistently continued for the teaching of Telegraphing by a practical operator who recognizes the obligations of a teacher to a pupil, arrangements have been completed which will enable those seeking such instruction to receive it during the

DAY OR EVENING,

upon reasonable terms. Students can enter at any time and receive instruction at such hours as may best suit their convenience. The course of instruction involves

OFFICE PRACTICE,

without additional charge.

Tuition, - - Forty Dollars,

without any limitation of time.

Those interested will please call at the College,

39 SOUTH TENTH ST., COR. CHESTNUT,

SECOND FLOOR, INMAN BUILDING.

CRAIG, FINLEY & ROWLEY, PRS. 10TH & CHESTNUT STS.

The timing was right for his return to education as well. The increasing pace of American economic expansion, coupled with revolutionary technological breakthroughs in office procedure represented by the telephone, telegraph, typewriter, and stenography gradually ended the slump in enrollments of the 1870s and paved the way for a resurgence in interest in commercial education in the 1880s.

Peirce College of Business held its first public commencement at the Academy of Music in 1882. Invited guests received the elegantly-engraved announcement (below) in 1885, the school's twentieth anniversary year.

Technology spawned advances in business practice, and education, in the 1870s. Demonstrations of the new Remington typewriter (pictured above from the Bettman Archives) astonished visitors to the Philadelphia Centennial, and may have influenced Dr. Peirce's decision to introduce typing courses in 1883. The school also briefly offered instruction in telegraphy (facing page.)

In 1881, Peirce renamed the Union Business College the Peirce College of Business. The following year, he moved the school to the Record Building at 917-919 Chestnut Street. The new building, hailed as a modern architectural wonder, was located next door to the equally magnificent new Post Office building. Peirce Business College classrooms, especially designed by Dr. Peirce, filled the entire fourth floor; the school also maintained a business office on the second floor. Interestingly, the school was in operation in the partially-completed structure before the building's owners, the publishers of the Philadelphia Record newspaper, could occupy the remaining floors. At the Record Building, "every convenience for [the students'] use known to the architecture or to the sanitation of the present day has been introduced," including electric lights, a passenger elevator, steam heat, "spacious" lavatories, and "closet-wardrobes."

Dr. Peirce's public accomplishments during the 1870s brought him heightened personal stature and social prestige. He turned these assets to the advantage of the school in many ways, including arranging weekly guest lectures by prominent local businessmen and political figures. In no way, perhaps, was this advantage more apparent than at commencement. On June 15, 1882, Peirce College of Business held its first public commencement at the Academy of Music. That year, Peirce began its tradition of bringing the finest local and national personalities to Philadelphia, and in the years that followed an ever-escalating list of luminaries, including governors, senators, and cabinet members graced the Peirce stage.

Below: The Record Building, third home of Peirce College of Business, circa 1890. Facing page: the school's shorthand and typewriting facilities as they appeared in 1900.

By the 1890s, the roster of Peirce commencement speakers had grown to include Andrew Carnegie, ex-presidents Benjamin Harrison and Grover Cleveland, and Police Commissioner of New York Theodore Roosevelt. The tradition would continue well into the twentieth century, with addresses by William Jennings Bryan, ex-president William Howard Taft, deposed leader of the Russian Provisional Government Alexander Kerensky, as well as a second appearance by Roosevelt.

In 1883, Dr. Peirce made the maneuver that would assure Peirce College continued and increasing success into the 20th century when he introduced the department of Shorthand and "Type-Writing." The novelty of these subjects, as well as a stubbornly prevalent negative attitude toward the employment of young women in business offices, kept attendance in this department low for the first few years. However, by 1888 Peirce's vision and patience were rewarded as total attendance climbed over 1000 for the first time, including over 300 women.

SHORTHAND AND TYPEWRITING DEPARTMENTS

Dr. Peirce had wanted to offer shorthand and typewriting for some time before 1883, but qualified instructors were scarce. The move to the Record building alleviated this problem, and enabled the school to offer these subjects for the first time. By a fortunate coincidence, Dr. Cyrus R. Morgan, Stenographic Commissioner of the Court of Common Pleas Number 4, held his office on the second floor of the Record Building. Morgan, whose office was equipped with typewriters, stenographic machines, and an experienced staff, agreed to provide equipment and instruction in these skills to Peirce students, presumably when not occupied by official duties.

Instruction at first was in hand-written stenographic systems, such as Pitman and Gregg. However, there was some dispute, at this early date, as to which system was most efficient.

1.

2.

3.

In 1893, Benjamin Harrison, whose term as President expired in March of that year, became the first of four ex-presidents to address a Peirce graduating class. Harrison praised the curriculum of Peirce School as "eminently practical."

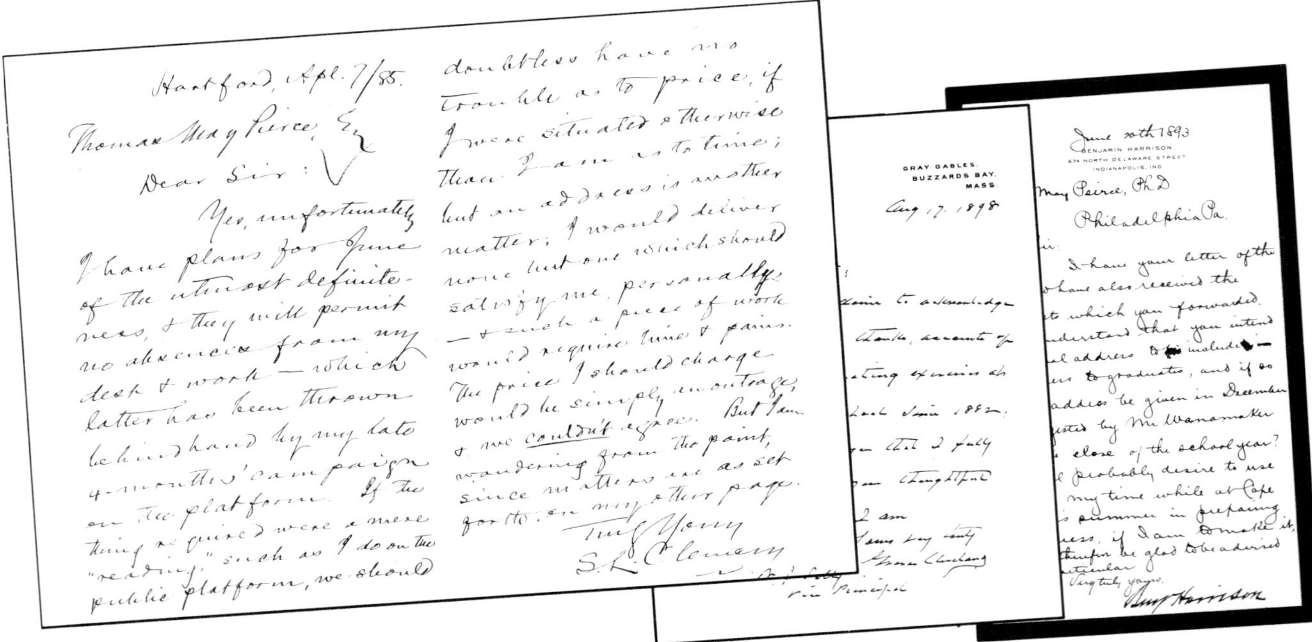

Hartford, Apl. 7/85.

Thomas May Peirce, Esq

Dear Sir:

Yes, unfortunately I have plans for June of the utmost definiteness, & they will permit no absences from my desk & work — which latter has been thrown behindhand by my late 4-months' campaign on the platform. If the thing required were a mere "reading," such as I do on the public platform, we should doubtless have no trouble as to price, if I were situated otherwise than I am as to time; but an address is another matter; I would deliver none but one which should satisfy me, personally — & such a piece of work would require time & pains. The price I should charge would be simply an outrage, & we couldn't agree. But I am wandering from the point, since matters are as set forth on my other page.

Truly Yours

S. L. Clemens

In 1900, Grover Cleveland, twice president of the U.S., addressed the Peirce commencement. Cleveland stated, "In my opinion, the particular type of education aimed at in the Peirce School has some important advantages over others."

4.

5.

6.

A partial gallery of Peirce commencement speakers includes: 1.) Theodore Roosevelt, 2.) Benjamin Harrison, 3.) Grover Cleveland, 4.) Alexander Kerensky, 5.) Andrew Carnegie, and 6.) William H. Taft. The Peirce Junior College Archives contains letters from many of these and other 19th and 20th century celebrities, some of which are reproduced below. In these regards, the school suffered one of its few disappointments in 1885 (facing page, bottom left) when Samuel Clemens, also known as Mark Twain, could not be persuaded to appear.

WILLIAM McKINLEY,
CANTON, OHIO.

March 18th. 1896.

Mr. W. J. Solly.
V.Principal, Peirce School.
917 Chestnut St.
Philadelphia, Pa.

My Dear Sir :-

Your proposition as repeated in your favor of the 14th. inst. is a very flattering one, but I must insist upon my declination. I hope sometime to have the pleasure of visiting your school, but I am so much occupied now as to make it out of the question for me to accept your invitation.

Yours very sincerely,

W [illegible] McKinley

WILLIAM H. TAFT
NEW HAVEN, CONN.

January 23, 1914.

My dear Mr. Moffett:

I have your letter of January 22nd, and thank you for your courtesy in sending me the clippings from the Philadelphia morning papers. I am very glad indeed to have them.

I note with interest what you say about my address. I am very glad to know that it met with the approval of those connected with the school. It afforded my much pleasure to have the opportunity of addressing the Peirce School and of speaking out the things which I really believe.

Yes, I found the proper enclosure in the envelope which you gave me at the League. $1000.00 — in one hundred dollar bills — have already taken up a note with it. Present my compliments to and regards. [illegible]

Sincerely yours,

Wm H Taft

Mr. L. B. Moffett,
Director, The Peirce School,
Philadelphia, Pennsylvania.

Police Department
of the City of New York.
300 Mulberry Street.

Board of Police Commissioners.
Theodore Roosevelt, President
Avery D. Andrews, Treasurer
Frederick D. Grant.
Andrew D. Parker.

New York. Aug. 18, 1896.

Mrs. T. M. Peirce,
Peirce School, 919 Chestnut St.,
Phila. Pa.

DearMadam:-

I thank you very much for sending me the cop of the Graduating Exercises; I shall read them with the utmost interest.

Yours very truly,

Theodore Roosevelt

In 1884, Peirce experimented with the exclusive use of the Stenograph, a new mechanical system, perhaps on Morgan's influence, very similar to court reporting machines in use a century later.

Like the experiment with the Stenograph, the arrangement with Morgan did not last long. By 1890, the school had its own equipment and staff for the teaching of shorthand and typewriting, and had settled on the "pen and pencil" Benn Pitman system of shorthand. In order to graduate, a shorthand student had to pass an examination involving five minutes of accurate shorthand notes from dictation at an average speed of 90 words per minute, and accurate transcription of the shorthand notes on the typewriter at an average speed of thirty words per minute. Dr. Peirce insisted that, unlike in other schools, the study of English and grammar be mandatory in the Shorthand and Typewriting Department.

"Only the standard and best being the rule at Peirce School, it is perhaps unnecessary to say that the system taught is Benn Pitman phonography in its purity-- 'The American System of Shorthand.'"

The high quality of Peirce graduates demanded the attention of local employers who deluged the school with applications to employable graduates and students. The school screened these requests carefully and recommended applicants. In effect, the college was operating a placement service, although it was reluctant to formalize this practice. Dr. Peirce continued to be explicit that he would not promise employment to anyone, but he noted that "The Dean [Thompson] spends more of his time in learning the details of situations to be filled, and in selecting the worthiest and likeliest student to succeed in the same, than on any other line of duty, excepting only the enrollment of new students."

By 1891, the departments of the school were reorganized to include the Banking and Business Department, the Bookkeep-

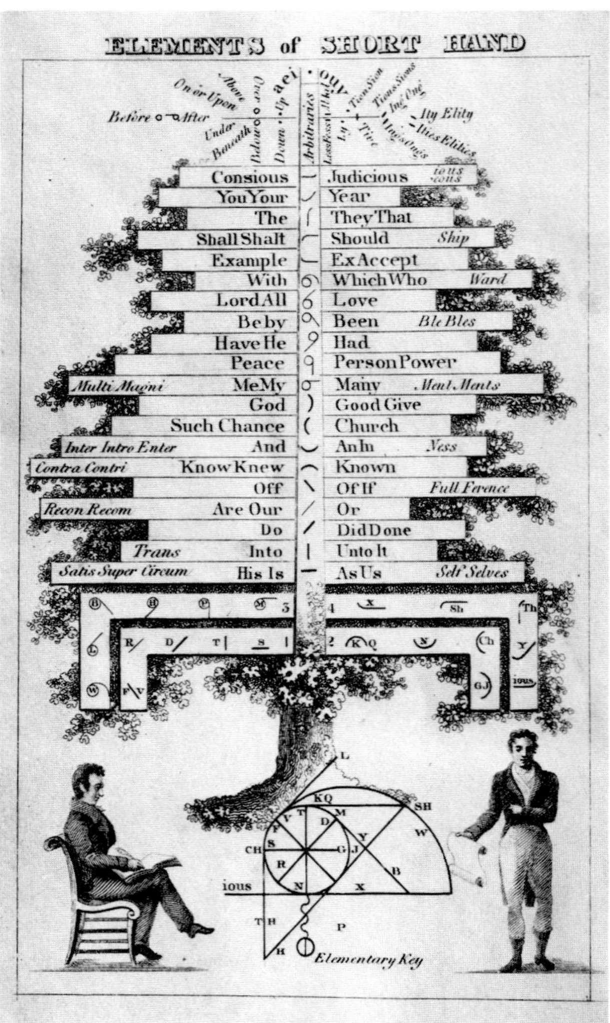

Above: Dr. Peirce and his second-floor office in the Record Building, circa 1895. Facing page: Frontispiece to an early treatise on Shorthand, published in Philadelphia in 1830. Some of the symbols were still in use over a century later.

ing Department, The Academic Department, the Graduating Department, and the Shorthand and Typewriting Department. This change, involving mostly cosmetic changes of titles, represented the end of the founding cycle in the evolution of the Peirce business curriculum, and resulted in a program that would remain untouched into the 1920s.

Of the changes, only the Graduating Department was new. Dr. Peirce found that few students were able to pass his stringent final examinations for graduation without a period of review. He therefore established the Graduating Department to formalize this process. The content of the department comprised a systematic review of all courses of the business program, with a particular emphasis on arithmetic.

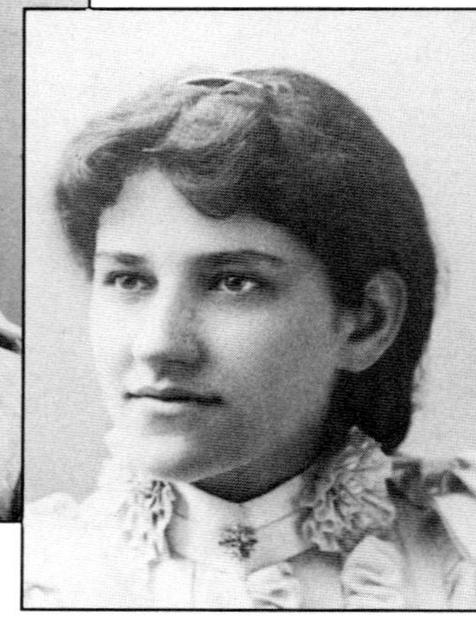

Purple, white, and gold,
Siss, boom, bah,
Three cheers, Peirce School,
Rah! Rah! Rah!

Alumni Organization

Although the Alumni Association of Peirce School was not formally established until 1892, the first stirrings of alumni organization occurred a year earlier. At the annual commencement exercises at the Academy of Music in 1891, a committee of students and alumni presented Thomas May Peirce with a school flag. This banner, in purple, white, and gold, led to the adoption of the school colors. Thomas Barlow, in presenting the banner to Dr. Peirce, said: "These colors, which I have the honor to present to you in behalf of your students and graduates and the alumni of this College, are intended to be expressive of our affectionate regard and a recognition of the just merit which should be accorded you."

On June 15, 1892, a group of enthusiastic graduates met in the Business Department of the school to form the Peirce College of Business Alumni Association. The formation of the Association was the work of seven graduates: J. E. M. Keller, William W. Rorer, Jennie W. Rogers, Sadie F. O'Neill, Charles H. Hoffman, Wilbur M. Frantz, and Ruth Peirce, all current Peirce faculty members, who organized the June 15 general meeting earlier that year. The purpose of the association, as stated in its by-laws, was "to promote social intercourse among the graduates of Peirce School and to aid the

From its inception in 1892, the Peirce Alumni Association has been a vigorous force in school life. Facing page, clockwise from top left: Wilbur M. Frantz, founding member and president in 1905; Irene Fellheimer and Mary E. H. McNeill, Peirce alumnae and faculty members, 1888; alumni gather for the "Tally-Ho Ride and Dance," 1902; and the graduating class of the week of April 16, 1888. Above, top to bottom: J. E. M. Keller, first president of the Alumni Association; William W. Rorer, founding member and president in 1897; and Ruth Peirce, daughter of Thomas May Peirce, faculty member, and alumni organizer.

Faculty in popularizing our Alma Mater." The Alumni Association soon became a lively social group. In addition to its annual banquets, its members formed a number of clubs, including the Peirce Alumni Cyclers, who joined a national enthusiasm for bicycling that swept the country at the turn of the century. The Cyclers established a club house at 3118 Diamond Street, which became the scene of many enjoyable social events during the club's brief history.

In 1893, Peirce College of Business was renamed Peirce School of Business and Shorthand. Despite this new title, in subsequent years the institution frequently referred to itself, even in catalogs and on letterhead, merely as "Peirce School." Class rooms were expanded "with the hope that, for this year at least, we will not be compelled to refuse admission to any one for lack of accommodations." Attendance now topped 1200.

Perhaps because of the criticism leveled at business schools by the academic community, Dr. Peirce was never comfortable with the word "college" in the school's title. At an Alumni Banquet in 1892, he foreshadowed this change. "The American Business College is an evolution. I am sorry, and always have been sorry, that the word 'college' ever

Alumni Banquet at the Hotel Walton, 1917. Facing page: An 1875 cartoon depicts the chaos that would result if women were admitted to the workplace.

became a part of the name of a mercantile or commercial school, but I found it in existence, and a certain definite idea was expressed by it, and I have been too conservative to change it; but as we get further along on the lines of progress and development which we have been following for over a quarter of a century, I hope some day to change the name of Peirce College of Business to Peirce School of Business."

Later that year, Ruth Peirce, fourth daughter of Thomas May Peirce, was placed in charge of the typewriting department of the school. Miss Peirce graduated from both the business course and the shorthand course in 1891, the only student up to that time to receive two diplomas at one commencement. Her accomplishment drew warm congratulations from Andrew Carnegie, the speaker that evening.

Women as Students at Peirce

The full curriculum of the Union Business College was open to women from its opening in 1865, although, for a number of reasons, few took advantage at this early date. The idea of practical, career-oriented education for women encountered a great deal of cultural resistance in the 19th century America. Except for a handful of elite, Ivy League colleges known collectively as the "seven sisters," higher education for women was virtually non-existent. In the rare instances that women did attend college they were expected to study classical subjects, such as art and literature, that were deemed appropriate to their domestic roles in child rearing and teaching.

The first three ladies to attend Peirce enrolled on September 21, 1865, only the third day of classes. Their names were Lettie F. Ziegler, Mary Lord, and Sue Laverell.

[Bettman Archives.]

Peirce School was at the forefront in providing career-oriented education for women. Although Dr. Peirce favored full opportunities for women, he approached the topic gingerly at first. Early catalogs heavily emphasized the propriety of the Union Business College's accommodations for female students. Separate entrance and classroom facilities, as well as a private dressing room provided "that attention and privacy, the want of which [women] have found an insuperable barrier to acquiring a business education."

In addition, the early Union Business College sponsored a separate Ladies' Institute of Art, under the direction of Miss A. A. Chapman, in which women might acquire such "elegant and useful" accomplishments as Drawing, Painting, Ornamental Painting on Glass, Grecian Painting, Hair or Wax Flowers and Fruits, Ornamental Leather Work, Photograph Painting, Elocution, Music, and French.

Dr. Peirce, however, was uncomfortable with the evident inequality of these arrangements, and began to reform them as early as 1866. The "privacy that propriety requires and delicacy expects," he decided, would be fulfilled by private entrances and dressing rooms, but not by separate teaching arrangements. Separate class facilities for women, "by removing [ladies] from the principal department of the college...necessarily involves less attention from teachers and the possession of fewer facilities," and prevented women from meaningful participation in the practical department. From that year on, all female business students at Union Business College occupied the same hall and used the same facilities "enjoyed by the gentlemen." Again, Peirce was well ahead of his time, anticipating arguments utilized by later generations to gain equal rights for all Americans.

In retrospect, Peirce was proud of his record on the issue of education for women. In 1893, he wrote: "The Business School was among the first to open its doors to women. I remember now with what caution and shyness I managed to get Peirce College's doors open for women, but we finally got it open; it remains open, and, so far as I am concerned, it will never be shut again. The Business School has multiplied the opportunities for women to gain a livelihood without unsexing themselves."

Enrollments up to 1894 were sometimes as much as 25% women.

Transitions

On May 16, 1896, Thomas Peirce died. He had been ill for some time, and last appeared at the school in February of that year. During much of his illness, Dr. Peirce maintained contact with the school,

The woman strolling past Peirce School in this photo, taken around 1920, exudes feelings of confidence and independence, qualities presumably acquired as a by-product of a Peirce education. Inset: Ruth Stong Peirce, Principal 1896-1898.

directing its operations via messenger from the family home at 1616 North Broad Street. Despite a two-months' recuperative stay in Florida that Spring, he never recovered. His widow, Ruth Stong Peirce, assumed the office of principal until her own death two years later.

With the death of Dr.Peirce, there was some concern about the future status and directions of the school. Alumni were relieved to learn that the school would continue under the Peirce name with Ruth S. Peirce as Principal. Mrs. Peirce had been a teacher before marrying Dr. Peirce (following the death of his first wife in 1870), and it was understood to be her husband's wish that she take the reins of the school. The school experienced a slight falling off in attendance following Dr. Peirce's death, due, it was speculated, to public concern whether the school would maintain its high standards under new leadership, but began another period of steady growth in 1899.

1887: Miss Jennie Rogers joined the staff as the school's first regular female instructor.

The school's own literature stressed the continuity of his ideas after his death. "A business school conducted upon the best educative lines for a period of thirty-one years by the same principal, a man of strong personality and a sound educator, must have impressed upon it a policy that has become a part of its very being. Peirce School, under Dr. Thomas May Peirce, its founder and principal, has achieved an ever-growing success. We assert with fullest confidence that its continuance under the same management and with the same faculty guarantees its continued success. It will aim, as in the past, to give the very best business training."

The next years would tell whether that promise of continuity would be borne out.

As school principal, Mary B. Peirce relied on the judgment of able Peirce School administrators and family friends. Pictured above, clockwise from top left: John A. Luman, John Wanamaker, and Louis B. Moffett.

Chapter 3
Peirce School of Business Administration

With the death of Ruth Stong Peirce in 1898, Mary Bisbing Peirce, eldest daughter of Thomas May Peirce, assumed the office and title of principal of Peirce School. Mary B. Peirce held this office for 62 years, presiding over some of the school's most prosperous years until her death in February, 1960.

Although well educated, holding diplomas from the Philadelphia High School for Girls and Dickinson College, Peirce had little formal teaching or business experience. Moreover, she was very conscious of the prejudice against women holding positions of power and public responsibility at that time. With the help and encouragement of John Wanamaker and Boise Penrose, both prominent Philadelphia businessmen and friends of her father, she accepted the post despite initial misgivings.

Mary Bisbing Peirce, Principal 1898-1960

To help overcome these difficulties, Mary Peirce relied heavily on the experienced and capable staff her father had assembled at the school, allowing such men as Louis B. Moffett and J. A. Luman, both long-time administrators at Peirce, freedom in the day-to-day operation of the school. As a further precaution, she adopted the practice of using only her initials, M. B., to disguise her femininity.

The turn of the 20th century was an exciting and rewarding time for Peirce School. The school that Mary Peirce inherited, largely through the foresight of her father, was a leader in commercial education, a position that placed it at the forefront of American progress.

The era of 1870-1900 had been one of tremendous growth in almost all aspects of American society. Paced by a steady stream of technological advance, exemplified most visibly by the rise of the railroads, this period was one of powerful industrial and commercial expansion. Huge industrial and financial empires, built by such men as Andrew Carnegie in steel, John D. Rockefeller in oil, and J. P. Morgan in finance, signaled the emergence of the major American corporation.

This new-found economic might, combined with the growth of the modern navy, enabled America to become, for the first time, a true world power in international commerce and diplomacy. Furthermore, as a result of the Spanish-American War, the United States acquired its first overseas territories in Cuba, Puerto Rico, and the Philippines. In describing these events, an early generation of historians referred to this era the "Gilded Age" or "Confident Era" of American history. Later observers, less sanguine as some of the negative social effects of industrialization became apparent, labeled this period as one of "Robber Barons" and thinly veiled American imperialism.

Set firmly in this context of American progress, Peirce School's leadership in commercial education afforded it growing national and international prominence. Accolades to the value of the school's methods came from near and afar. In 1899, the school earned a silver medal and a diploma for its exhibit at the National Export Exposition in Philadelphia. The Peirce exhibit took the novel form of a composite classroom displaying elements of Peirce instruction: desks, cabinets, and equipment from the business and typewriting departments facing a blackboard covered with penmanship and shorthand characters.

The following year, Peirce School was awarded a gold medal for its exhibit at the Universal Exhibition at Paris, and "in recognition of its pioneer work in business education and its influence among business leaders at the turn of the century." Peirce was one of only six American business schools selected to be represented at the Paris exposition. The Peirce exhibit included photographs of the school and classrooms, samples of business forms and correspondence executed by students, a large penmanship display, and a description of the Benn Pitman system of phonography written in shorthand and typescript, with a French translation by Thomas May Peirce, Jr. Peirce's showing at Paris attracted international attention. Antoine Siniavsky, Director of l'Ecole de Commerce of Belostok, Russia was so impressed that he requested the loan of part of the exhibit in order that he might introduce some of the Peirce methods in Russian schools.

Peirce exhibits garnered national and international praise at the turn of the century. Facing page, top: Awards from the National Export Exposition, Philadelphia, 1899, and the Universal Exhibition, Paris, 1900. Bottom: The Peirce School exhibit at the National Export Exposition, also shown at Paris.

NATIONAL EXPORT EXPOSITION
AWARDED BY THE NATIONAL EXPORT EXPOSITION TO
PEIRCE SCHOOL
PHILADELPHIA, PA.
ON RECOMMENDATION OF THE FRANKLIN INSTITUTE
PHILADELPHIA
1899
RÉPUBLIQUE FRANÇAISE

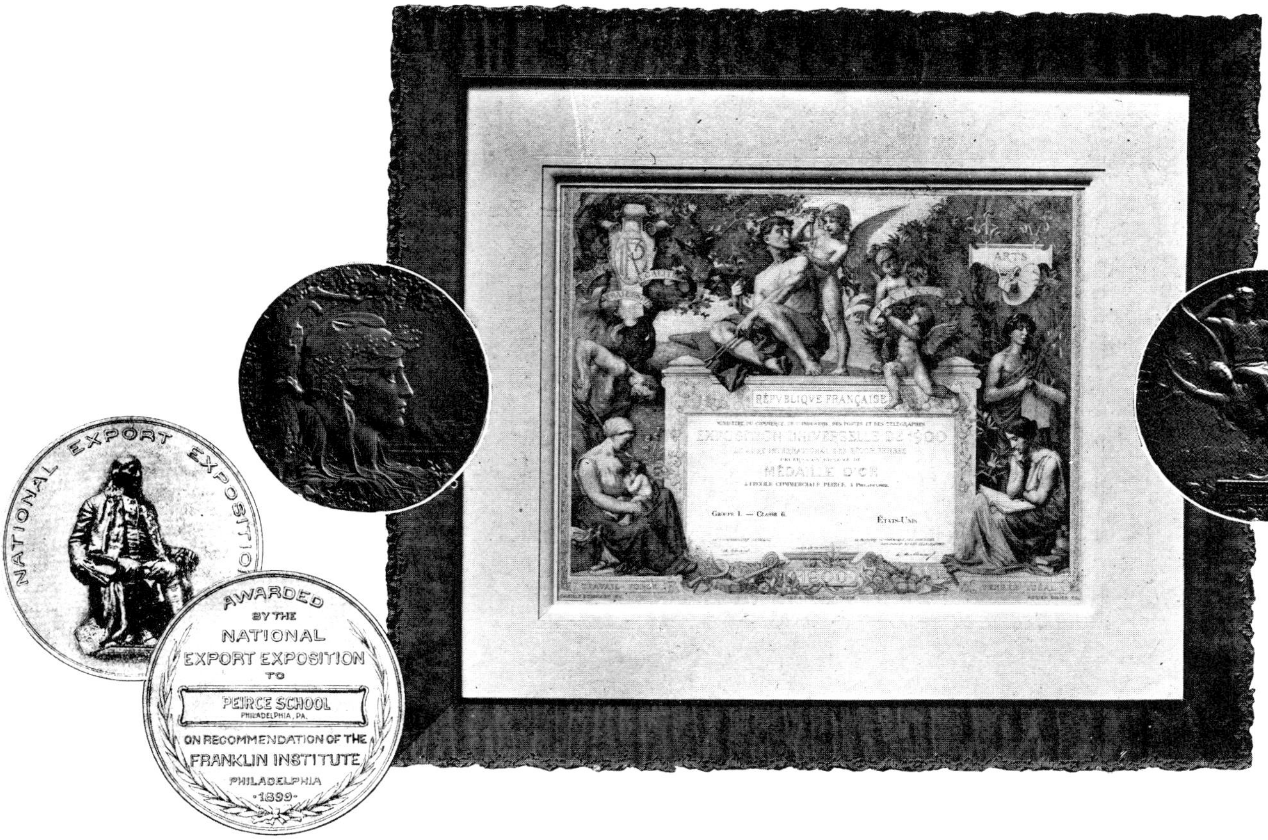

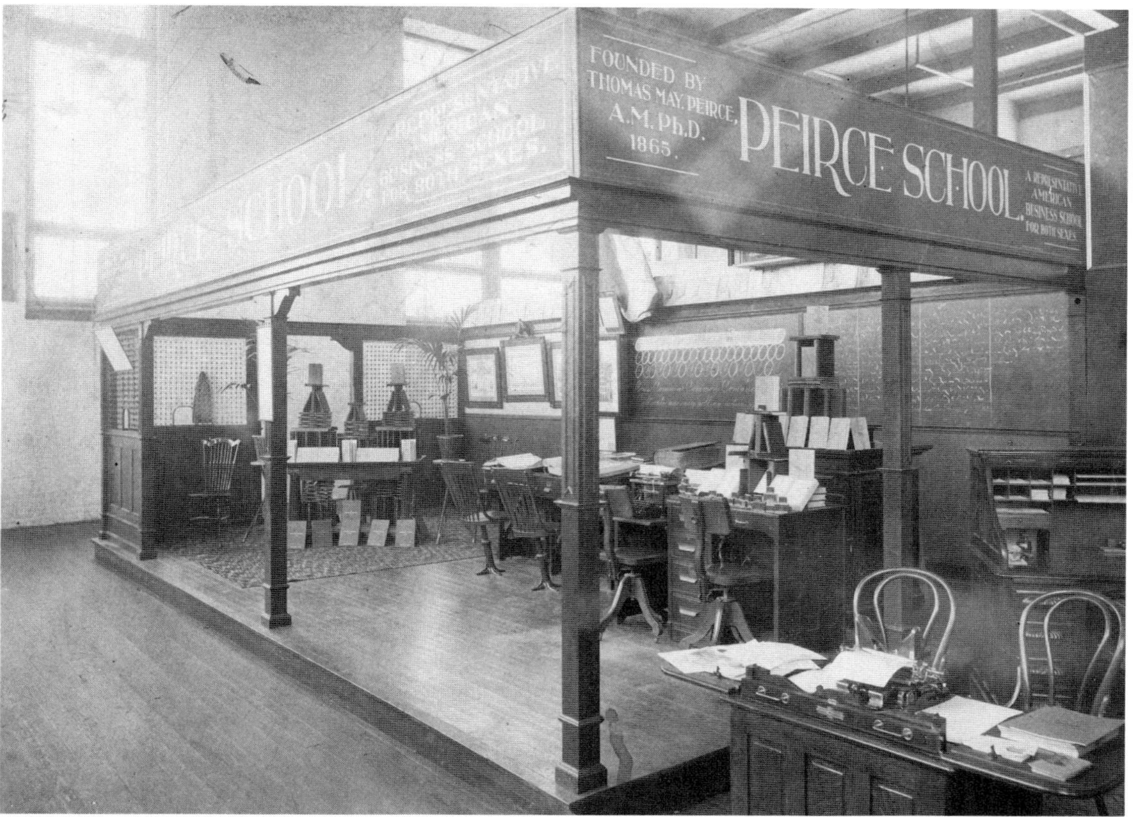

FOUNDED BY
THOMAS MAY PEIRCE,
A.M. Ph.D.
1865.
PEIRCE SCHOOL.
A REPRESENTATIVE AMERICAN BUSINESS SCHOOL FOR BOTH SEXES

BUSINESS EDUCATION
AT THE
PAN-AMERICAN EXPOSITION
Represented by
Albany Business College, Albany, N.Y.
Bryant & Stratton Business College, Buffalo.
Metropolitan Business College, Chicago.
Packard Commercial School, New York.
Peirce School, Philadelphia.
Spencerian Commercial School, Cleveland.
BUSINESS COLLEGES.
BUSINESS COLLEGES.
Exhibits above from
PEIRCE SCHOOL
PHILADELPHIA, PA.
PACKARD COMMERCIAL SCHOOL
NEW YORK CITY
ALBANY BUSINESS COLLEGE
ALBANY, N.Y.
Exhibits above from
SPENCERIAN COMMERCIAL SCHOOL
CLEVELAND, O.
BRYANT & STRATTON BUSINESS COLLEGE
BUFFALO, N.Y.
METROPOLITAN BUSINESS COLLEGE
CHICAGO, ILL.

In 1901, Peirce School won yet another award for its exhibit at the Pan-American Exposition in Buffalo. While visiting Buffalo that year, President William McKinley was assassinated, and Vice President Theodore Roosevelt assumed the presidency. In 1897, as Police Commissioner of New York, Roosevelt had addressed the Peirce School commencement.

Facing page: The Peirce exhibit was prominent among six business schools and colleges at the Buffalo Pan-American Exposition, 1901. Below: A billboard invites attendance at Peirce, and a montage of stamps and trading tokens from the school's role-playing Banking and Business Department.

Mary Peirce did not allow these accolades to engender complacency at the school. In a continuing effort to expand the reach and usefulness of the institution, the school continued to offer new and innovative programs. In 1901, a course in advertising was established in the night school under the direction of E. St. Elmo Lewis. This course was "intended to meet the needs of merchants, manufacturers and other proprietors who are advertisers of their own business, and of salesmen, bookkeepers, stenographers, and other employees who desire to increase their earning capacity. It also affords a thorough preparation for those who desire to enter the field as advertising agents or specialists."

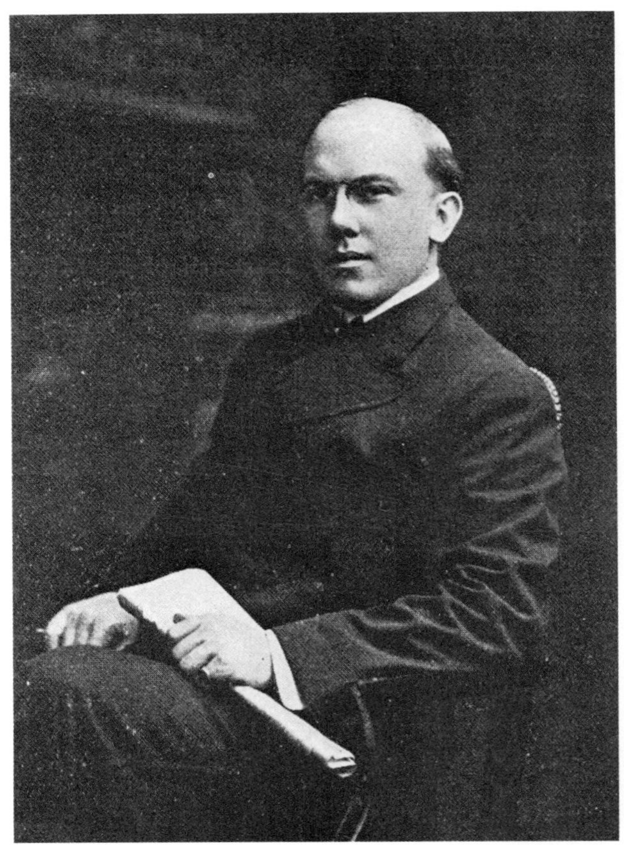

An ornate brochure (below) announced Peirce School's first course in advertising, under the charge of E. St. Elmo Lewis (above right.)

The following year, Peirce organized a Spanish-American Department to attract students from Latin-American countries. Although Peirce had been admitting Hispanic students for some years, the establishment of this department marked the beginning of a concerted effort to recruit students from this area, reflecting the tenor of the times.

Sinceramente
A. Somoza
1939

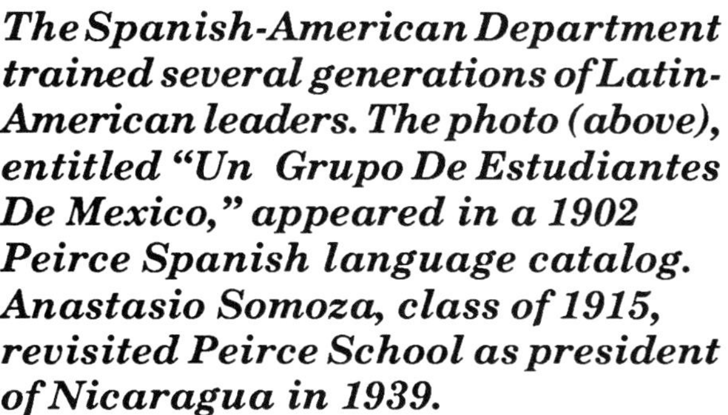

The Spanish-American Department trained several generations of Latin-American leaders. The photo (above), entitled "Un Grupo De Estudiantes De Mexico," appeared in a 1902 Peirce Spanish language catalog. Anastasio Somoza, class of 1915, revisited Peirce School as president of Nicaragua in 1939.

The department was in charge of Manuel Vera Estanol, a native of Mexico. Students entered the regular departments as soon as they acquired "a working knowledge of English." Peirce also introduced courses in the study of the Spanish language at this time. Among the notable graduates of the Spanish-American Department was Anastasio Somoza, class of 1915, who assumed the presidency of his native Nicaragua in 1937.

The Spanish-American Department became one of Mary Peirce's special projects. She felt the responsibility for the care of these foreign students keenly, frequently meeting arriving students at the dock. She would often look after their arrangements personally, providing rooms in her own home and personal loans if necessary until the students became comfortable and settled in Philadelphia. In later years, Miss Peirce's interest in Latin-American affairs earned her a seat on the board of governors of the Washington-based Pan-American Association.

The Information Department "is maintained not only for the benefit of its graduates and former students, but for the general public as well, and no charge of any kind is made for its services."

In 1904, the school, which by this time occupied two and one-half floors at the Record Building, secured the remainder of the second floor (its third altogether) and enlarged its library. The school, which now occupied half the total space in the building, (the entire second, third, and fourth floors) also added a private entrance at the post-office corner of the building leading directly to elevators to the upper floors.

The new space on the second floor was converted into a "reading room and social hall" to be open continuously from noon to 9:30 P.M. Peirce did this for the benefit of the increasing number of boarding students, to afford them someplace other than their rooms to spend their free time. The room was equipped with daily newspapers and magazines, a piano, and facilities for chess, checkers, and "similar games." The library was also open to students at these times. To insure a wholesome environment, ladies were not permitted in the room after 5 P.M. The room was also made available, upon special arrangement, for monthly meetings of student clubs.

In 1907, Peirce completed its first comprehensive survey of its alumni, and the impressive results came as a surprise even to the school itself. Of 1451 male respondents who had been in the business world 10 or more years, over 1000 were sole proprietors of a business, or held top executive positions with banking, manufacturing, or commercial firms.

Views of the Record Building circa 1904. Facing page, left: the Peirce School entrance; (right), the library.

"The mission of Peirce School is not to train its students to become bookkeepers or stenographers. Its courses of study, it is true, include bookkeeping and other commercial branches, but these are simply a means to an end. The true mission of the school is to give its students the general education that will prepare them to become the business leaders of the future."

Mary B. Peirce, in addition to regular administrative duties, took particular pride in maintaining Peirce's record of presenting eminent speakers on its commencement platform. Many of these gentlemen remarked that it was only through the tactful persuasion and persistency of Miss Peirce that they agreed to appear.

Woodrow Wilson, then President of Princeton University, was scheduled to address the 43rd graduating class in December, 1908. After having originally agreed, however, Wilson withdrew. Undaunted and unwilling to accept a lesser figure, Mary Peirce engineered a coup by securing William Jennings Bryan, regarded by most as the finest orator of his time, to appear instead. At the last minute, however, Bryan also begged off, cabling Mary Peirce from Chicago to claim that he was too ill to perform. Refusing to have her plans, and the expectations of thousands of Philadelphians, ruined again, Mary Peirce boarded the all-night train to Chicago, confronted Bryan personally, and convinced him to appear as scheduled.

The William Jennings Bryan appearance was a major local event, and one of the most outstanding of the many successful Peirce commencements. As usual on these occasions, the Academy was full to its 3000 seat capacity. Several thousand Philadelphians, eager to hear the great orator, had to be turned away at the door. Peirce commencements lent the school a stature in the local community beyond even its impressive educational accomplishments. The editors of the January, 1909 Alumni Journal, while apologetically commenting on the excitement caused by the Bryan speech and the disappointment suffered by those unable to gain entry, aptly summarized Peirce's position after 43 successful years: "The school...greatly regrets that there is no building in Philadelphia of sufficient capacity to accommodate all its friends."

William Jennings Bryan

Chauncey M. Depew, U.S. Senator from New York, exhorted Peirce graduates to "Stick, Dig, and Save" in 1902.

For many years, Peirce School had served as an informal reference source to the community, frequently resolving questions ranging from spelling and word usage to questions of accounting and business strategies. In 1908, Peirce formalized this service with the establishment of the Peirce School Information Bureau. "Inquiries on minor points may be made by telephone," the school said, "but where the question requires research and investigation, the inquiry should be made by mail." The Peirce School telephone number was Walnut 153.

Peirce was very selective when hiring faculty, always choosing candidates with impeccable credentials, and, most importantly, practical experience in their lines. In addition to its regular classroom lectures, Peirce arranged to have monthly guest lectures by prominent local experts in business-related occupations. In 1907, for example, guest lectures on various business topics were given by John Wanamaker, Edward T. Stotesbury, head of Drexel and Company and a graduate of the first class of the Union Business College in 1866, Theodore C. Search, then head of the John B. Stetson Company, president of the Pennsylvania Museum and School of Industrial Art, and founder of the Philadelphia Textile School (in later years, the Philadelphia College of Textiles and Science), and George Edward Reed, D.D., Ll.D, president of Dickinson College, among others. These Friday afternoon lectures, with the school orchestra entertaining during intermissions and breaks, became a tradition at Peirce.

The Peirce School Orchestra, led by Professor Alvin C. Kriebel (center row, seated in chair), in 1912.

In 1909, Peirce School established its own commercial museum in its reading room at the Record Building, to be used in conjunction with its commercial geography course. The collection, in true conformity to the school's tradition of learning by seeing and doing, was designed to supplement student's textbook knowledge of the manufacturing process by illustrating the stages of production of various staple commodities from raw materials to finished goods. The chocolate industry, for example, was represented by photographs of a cocoa tree, actual pods and cocoa beans, description and illustrations of the process by which these raw materials are refined, and samples of by-products and finished chocolate. The collection was housed in ten tall, glass-fronted exhibit cases. Each hand-built cabinet featured a wood carving depicting a device or phase of industry: a locomotive, ocean steamer, oil derrick, factory, tree, sheaf of wheat, a steer's head, and a book.

In December of that year, The Philadelphia Board of Public Education honored Dr. Thomas May Peirce for his career in local education by dedicating the new school at Twenty-third and Cambria Streets in his name. At ceremonies that evening, attended by many local officials, the Peirce family presented a large oil portrait of Thomas May Peirce to be hung in the school lobby. That same year, the school achieved accreditation by the educational authorities in "several States."

In 1910, Peirce announced its first Secretarial Course "designed particularly to prepare young women for secretarial positions, although it will be open to men as well." The course, which combined the entire existing shorthand course with elements of the business course, included such topics as commer-

This portrait, donated by members of the Peirce family, graced the lobby of the new Thomas May Peirce Public School. The Philadelphia Board of Education honored Dr. Peirce by naming this public school after him in 1909.

cial law, accounting, and business forms and customs. Peirce's language in announcing the course subtly reflected the second-class status that women still endured in American society: "The position of Private Secretary carries with it not only attractive emoluments, but also much dignity. Women seem particularly fitted to fill such posts, when properly trained. Their alertness, willingness and loyalty are seldom called into question. With a knowledge of the technique of their work, acquired at Peirce School, many become, in a comparatively short time, among the most valued and highly paid employees."

On the other hand, while men were not discouraged from taking the course, the school recommended that men should also take the entire business course, since "it should be the ambition of every young man to eventually become the head of the business."

By 1915, Peirce School approached an even higher level of success under Principal Mary B. Peirce. Enrollments were climbing steadily. Nearly 400 Latin-Americans had attended the Spanish-American Department since its inception in 1902. Demand for Peirce graduates was higher than ever before, with the Peirce Placement Office receiving between 1500 and 2000 requests for Peirce graduates annually. One conspicuous result of this success was a lack of space. The Record Building, which had seemed spacious thirty years before, could no longer accommodate the growing school, and Peirce School began to search for a new and larger location.

The Thomas May Peirce Public School, Twenty-third and Cambria Streets, Philadelphia, circa 1909.

In 1887, Simon Guggenheim graduated from Peirce College, one of four Guggenheim brothers to attend Peirce. Guggenheim later became the first Peirce alumni to be elected to the U.S. Senate from the state of Colorado.

This is the best penmanship that I can execute at the time of commencing my studies at Pierce's Business College January 6th 1885. Simon Guggenheim

Thomas May Peirce
Dear Sir, This is a fair sample of my penmanship, after one months decided effort to improve it. Hoping to receive the Reward of Merit, I am
Yours truly,
S Guggenheim
October 29, 1885

"Before" and "After" specimens were a staple element of Peirce School penmanship instruction. In 1912, the school distributed hundreds of these specimens collected over the years to their authors as souvenirs. By the time of his graduation, Simon Guggenheim (left and above) undoubtedly learned the correct spelling of "Peirce." Guggenheim's brothers Benjamin, Murray, and Daniel also attended Peirce School.

News of the Titanic disaster shook Peirce School in 1912. As noted in this page from the Peirce Alumni Journal, former students George Widener and Benjamin Guggenheim were among those lost in the sinking.

This is the best penmanship that
I can execute at the time of
commencing my studies at
Pierce's Business College
October 10th 1881 George D. Widener

These specimens were written by the late George D. Widener, of Philadelphia, while a student at Peirce School. Mr. Widener was among the many distinguished men to meet death on the Titanic. It will be remembered that another distinguished alumnus of Peirce School, Benjamin Guggenheim, of New York, was also on the ship. The school recently found Mr. Widener's specimens, and had the pleasure of sending them to his father, Mr. P. A. B. Widener, the well-known financier.

Thomas May Peirce
Dear Sir: This is a fair sample
of my penmanship after one month's
decided effort to improve it. Hoping to
secure the College Reward of Merit, I am
Yours truly
February 1st 1882 Geo. D. Widener

This is the best penmanship that
I can execute at the time of
commencing my studies at
Pierce's Business College
January 2. 1883 Ben Guggenheim

Thomas May Peirce
Dear Sir: This is a fair sample
of my penmanship after one month's
decided effort to improve it.
Hoping to receive the College
Reward of Merit, I am
Yours truly
Ben Guggenheim
Phila 3/2/83

In 1915, fifty years after its founding, Peirce School moved to spacious new quarters at 1420 Pine Street, Philadelphia. Below: a 1915 sketch of the building by artist Frank H. Taylor, showing the roof-top sporting area. Facing page, top to bottom: one of the new classrooms, the reception room, and the entrance hall.

Chapter 4
Pine Street, West of Broad

In 1915, Peirce School moved to its present location at 1420 Pine Street, Philadelphia. Coincidentally, this move occurred on the fiftieth anniversary of its founding in 1865. This building, built in 1898 by Henry Hobart Brown to house his DeLancey School for Boys, represented an investment by Peirce of over $500,000.

Peirce School considered the building to be well worth the investment. The modern, seven-story structure contained its own basement power plant providing electricity for the entire building, spacious office and class room facilities, a two-floor gymnasium and indoor running track said to be "unsurpassed" by any other in the country, male and female locker room facilities with "shower baths," a two-lane bowling alley, elevators, "sterilized and filtered" drinking water delivered to a fountain on each floor, and assembly, club, and library rooms. The Carlisle street entrance was reserved for the use of students only; the general public used the Pine Street entrance. The roof was caged, allowing it to be used for tennis, basketball, and other recreations. For the first time, the school opened its own restaurant on the fourth floor for students and staff.

The school moved despite misgivings held in some quarters that the new location, being far removed from the main "bright light" shopping district of Ninth and Chestnut Streets, would exert a negative impact on attendance, especially in the evening classes. These fears dissipated almost at once. By October, the night school had enrolled over 700 pupils, slightly more than the previous year's total at the Record Building.

While less luxurious, to be sure, than Handel and Haydn Hall, the new building nevertheless provided an elegant educational atmosphere. Facilities included (at left) a reading room, (below) an auditorium, (facing page, top) a library, and (bottom) a club room.

The move enabled Peirce School to offer its first classes in physical education. Above: A view of the Philadelphia skyline enlivens a class in calisthenics. Facing page: Physical training instructor William J. Herrmann (wearing a suit, far right) poses with a gymnastics class. The sixth/seventh floor gymnasium boasted a suspended running track, visible in the upper portion of the photograph.

School officials praised the tranquility and convenience of the Pine Street location where, although "within two squares" of such landmarks as the Union League, Stock Exchange, Bellevue-Stratford, and Ritz-Carlton hotels, the "absence of noise, dirt, and dust" provided a more "scholastic atmosphere" than obtained on Chestnut Street.

Gymnastic and locker room facilities at the new building allowed Peirce School to offer "physical training" classes for the first time, under the auspices of William J. Herrmann of the Herrmann Physical Training Institute. Instruction was offered in "body building, developing, respiratory, setting up, calisthenics, gymnastics, and recreative exercises." In announcing the classes, school officials stressed that gymnastic work was strictly optional, and the school had no intention of using the classes as a springboard to competition in inter-collegiate sports.

That same year, the Peirce School Building and Loan Association was formed by members of the Alumni Association and faculty "to assist boys and girls, who are just starting their business careers, affording them a safe investment for their surplus earnings which will yield them a satisfactory income, and to teach them the rudiments of economy."

Peirce School in World War I

When the United States entered World War I in 1917, Peirce, freshly renamed Peirce School of Business Administration, initiated a number of special programs and activities to help the country face its national emergency.

Soon after the declaration of war, Peirce introduced a series of special "War Courses" designed to help fill the demand for clerical workers in both the public and the draft-depleted private sectors. The courses, between ten and thirty weeks in length, were primarily designed to train women to fill war-created vacancies. However, the courses were also extended, free of charge, to local branches of the armed services, notably the Army Ordnance Field Service and Naval Reserves, to train war-time recruits in typewriting and other trappings of the modern military bureaucracy.

At the same time, Peirce School offered the American Red Cross and the Women's Liberty Loan Committee full use of the school's auditorium and other facilities. The roof of the school became a drilling area. Students and faculty formed a Liberty Loan Bond Committee, subscribing a total of nearly $230,000 to government coffers during the course of the war.

Peirce School mobilized its resources to aid the war effort during World War I. At left, Peirce "boys" muster on Pine Street before going "over there."

Over 1000 Peirce graduates and students saw active service in the armed forces, with at least twenty-three giving their lives in the line of duty.

One of the most successful of the Peirce School war-time activities was a group of female alumnae and students organized by Mary B. Peirce known as the Comfort Kit Club. The club assembled over 250 "comfort kits," each containing a sweater, socks, handkerchiefs, writing materials, washcloths and soap, candles, combs, steel "trench mirrors," games, postcards, and candy and distributed them to "Peirce boys" and other needy soldiers at the front. In addition, club members stitched leather "trench jackets" out of individual kid gloves, and donated them to the ambulance and aviation services.

After the war, Peirce continued to do "its bit" by participating in the "rehabilitation" of returning soldiers into peaceful pursuits. Between 1919 and 1926, over 800 war veterans, placed at Peirce by the U.S.Veterans Bureau, studied business and accounting at the school. Attendance, swollen by the influx of World War veterans, reached a record 3000 in 1920, and the school reluctantly converted its splendid gymnasium for classroom use.

Copyright by Committee on Public Information

The Fighting Army and The Working Army

Recruits are needed for both. And efficient workers require intensive training no less than efficient fighters.

Peirce School trains for either army. More than a thousand Peirce School graduates are in the service. They hold every important rank from Brigadier-General to private. Their Peirce training has proved its worth.

Peirce School graduates are the "commissioned officers" of the business world. They command the responsible positions—and the rapid advancement of Peirce graduates is a Philadelphia business proverb.

Every Peirce course is a thorough training to cope with the business problems of today. Courses include Banking, Accounting, Business Management, Commercial Law, Business Correspondence and similar practical subjects. Many young women are training for Red Cross, Government, Emergency Business and Secretarial positions at Peirce School.

Splendid modern school building—one of the finest in America.

Send for 54th Year Book

America's Foremost Business School

Peirce School
of Business Administration
Pine Street, West of Broad, Phila., Pa.

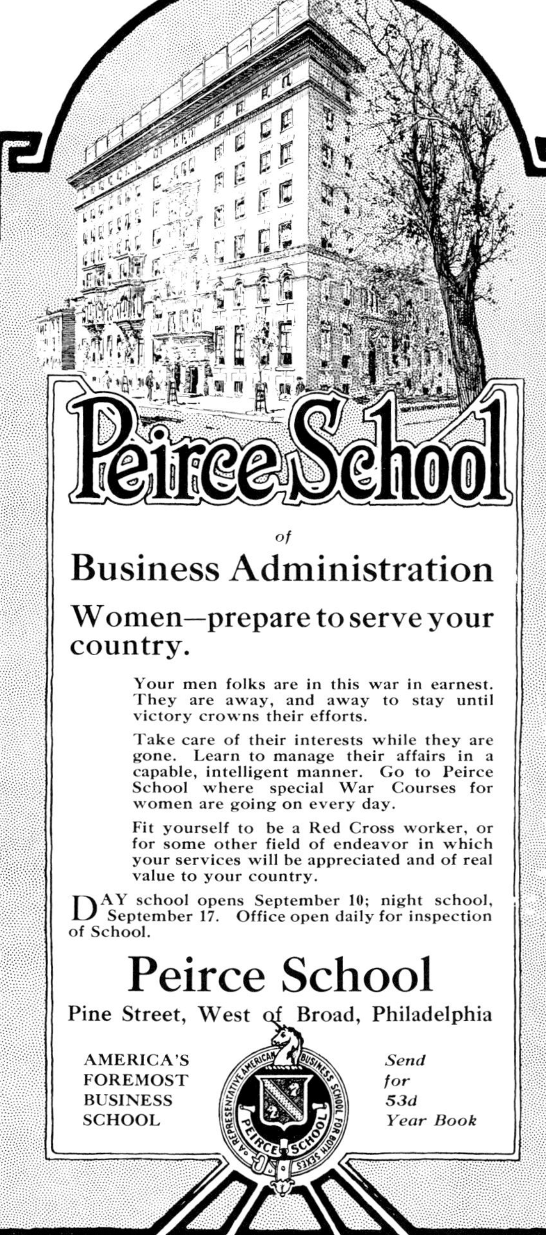

Uncle Sam is Spending Millions in *Training Men*

Training—The Gospel of Efficiency—has been preached to great effect by the Government in the Officers' Training Camps. From morning until night—ten hours a day—men are prepared to become leaders.

What have you done to become a leader in business? Are you trained? Can you manage an office—direct workers—show them how to do their work accurately and quickly?

Peirce School trains young men and women to become the best in their field. That is why most Peirce graduates are proprietors of their own businesses within ten years after graduation.

EVERY Course at Peirce School is the result of fifty-three years of teaching experience.

Day School opens September 10; Night School, September 17
Office open daily for inspection of School

Peirce School

of

Business Administration

AMERICA'S FOREMOST BUSINESS SCHOOL

Pine Street, West of Broad, Philadelphia

(*Send for 53d Year Book*)

The Peirce advertisements on these pages demonstrate the importance of business education to full-scale mobilization in a modern overseas war.

Curriculum Development

In 1920, the school announced a restructuring and expansion of its curriculum, the most extensive modernization effort undertaken in many years. Events of the previous thirty years mandated the changes. Since the 1890s, many four-year college and universities had established programs in business and finance, among them Drexel University and the Wharton School of the University of Pennsylvania in Philadelphia. In addition, professions like accounting, previously subsumed under bookkeeping, were rapidly professionalizing and acquiring their own separate identities.

To keep pace with these developments, Peirce initiated a two-year option in its Business Administration curriculum. The new course was designed to be of university caliber. In the Peirce tradition of efficient and practical education, the course offered a college-level business program stripped of the university's general education or "cultural" requirements. The new course expanded around the core of the traditional Peirce business course, adding advanced sections of older courses as well as new courses in accounting, commerce and transportation, investments, cost accounting, business psychology, and income tax accounting.

The school also announced a two-year major program, closely paralleling the business administration course, which offered a specialization in accounting and preparation for the newly-established Certified Public Accountant examination. In addition, the courses in salesmanship, which had been added the year before, secretarial training, shorthand, and teachers' training were strengthened. Students might also take special, shorter courses in any discipline, courses designed as preparation for the Civil Service examination, or fashion a program of study tailored to suit their specific needs.

Peirce continued to refine its curricula through the next several years, with the establishment in 1923 of a course in Real Estate Law and Conveyencing in the Evening School. Two years later, a Business Administration Course for College Graduates was created in the day school.

Classroom Views, Circa 1920. Left and facing page, top: secretarial classrooms. Facing page, bottom: a class in business mathematics.

Peirce School on the Air

On April 29, 1922, Peirce's first radio broadcast, "Selecting a Vocation" by Harry E. Bartow of the Peirce faculty, launched a long-standing tradition of public service broadcasts by the school in Philadelphia. The show aired on station WDAR, which was owned and operated by Lit Brothers department store. Only two years earlier, commercial radio had gotten off to a controversial and uncertain start in the United States with a single station, KDKA, in Pittsburgh. The program was the first in a series of weekly "educational talks" delivered by members of the Peirce School faculty.

The series was a success, and in the years that followed Peirce continued to provide WDAR, its successor WLIT, and the public with innovative programming. Later in 1922, in an extension of the Information Bureau service the school provided, Peirce added a question and answer feature to its weekly broadcasts, answering queries "of general interest" over the air waves and soliciting listeners' suggestions for topics of future shows.

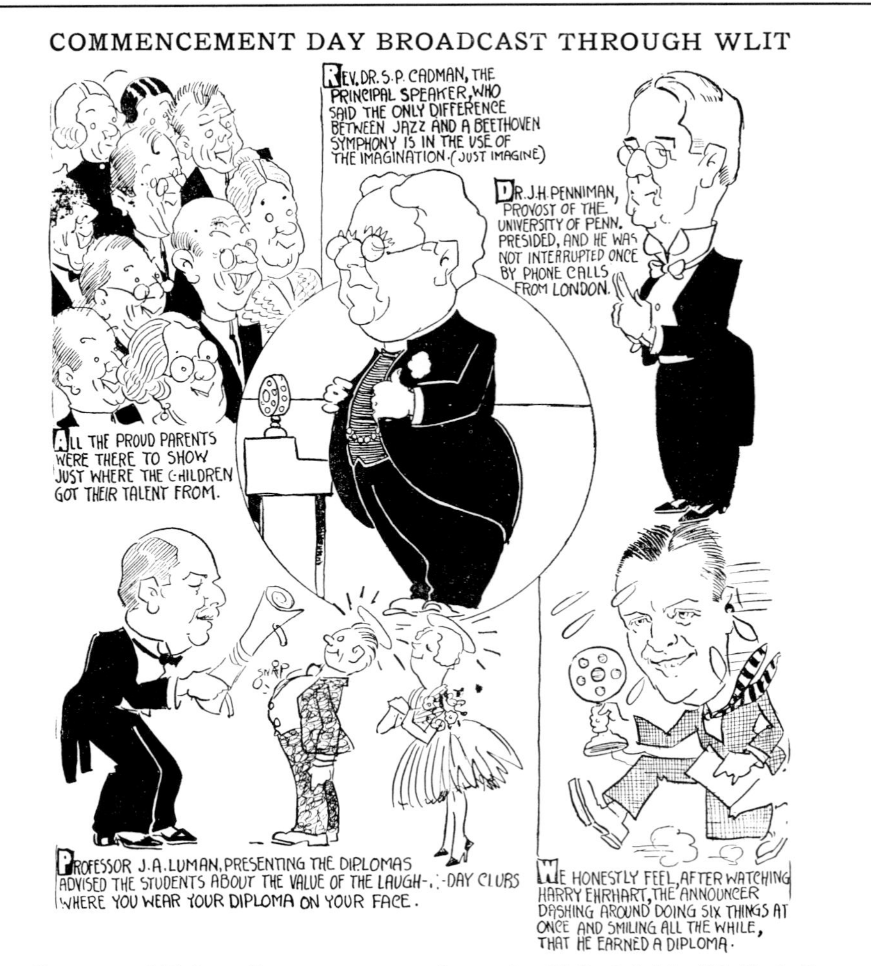

Cartoon of Peirce Commencement from the Philadelphia "Bulletin" of January 29, 1927

Peirce also looked to radio to ease its annual problem of arranging seating at its popular commencement exercises. In 1924, WDAR broadcast the Honorable James Beck's address to the 58th graduating class on location from the Academy of Music, a practice that was repeated in ensuing years. This event was believed to be the first broadcast of its kind.

Perhaps the most popular of all Peirce School programming during the 1920s, however, were its annual spelling bees and radio shorthand contests. Both invited audience participation. Listeners entered the shorthand contests by submitting their transcriptions of a carefully constructed passage delivered over the radio. Winners, in such qualifying categories as "pupil" "teacher," "stenographer," and "long distance" (perhaps reflecting the handicap suffered by participants in such fringe reception areas as Easton, Pennsylvania and Trenton, New Jersey), were selected according to the faithfulness of their copy. At one point, two newspapers, the North American and the Record, who participated in sponsorship of the spelling and shorthand contests, received over 3000 entries per day.

As the popularity of radio surged in the mid-1920s, Peirce expanded its programming to four days per week. Two series, "Going Into Business With a Small Capital," and "Philadelphia Leads America," featured prominent local businessmen speaking on business topics. In cooperation with the Philadelphia Sesqui-Centennial Commission, throughout 1925 and 1926 Peirce sponsored a series of "Sesqui-Centennial Bulletins," which included interviews with many of the exhibition's commissioners and foreign exhibitors. A fourth series, "The Peirce School Weekly Survey of Business and Employment Conditions," conducted by H.E. Bartow, elicited much comment at its inception in 1926. Interest in the series among Philadelphia businessmen ran so high that requests for transcripts flooded the Peirce switchboards, and the school honored hundreds of such standing requests weekly during the show's five-year run.

Radio
Shorthand Contest
Certificate

Awarded by

PEIRCE SCHOOL OF
BUSINESS ADMINISTRATION
PHILADELPHIA—PENNSYLVANIA

to

Charlotte Beck

For Qualifying Transcript at
80 words a minute
submitted in the First Philadelphia
Radio Shorthand Contest broadcast
from WLIT on May 16, 1929.

Louis B. Moffett
Director

H. E. Bartow
Secretary

Peirce School was quick to recognize the power and popularity of radio. Peirce broadcasts, introduced in 1922, included (facing page) commencement addresses, (left) shorthand and spelling contests, and other public service programming.

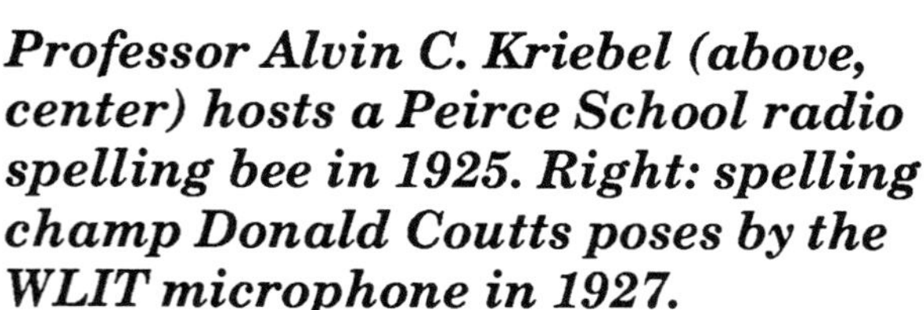

Professor Alvin C. Kriebel (above, center) hosts a Peirce School radio spelling bee in 1925. Right: spelling champ Donald Coutts poses by the WLIT microphone in 1927.

In 1926, Peirce School entered the sphere of intercollegiate sports, fielding teams in basketball, baseball, and track. Although Peirce students had competed informally in sports at various times in the past (for example, a baseball team composed mainly of World War I veterans played in a league organized by the Veterans Bureau in 1920), these teams were the first to compete officially under the banner of the purple, white, and gold. The teams were successful almost from the start. All sported winning records their first few years, culminating with a City

Above: Peirce School Veterans League Baseball Team, 1920. Below right: the 1921-1922 Basketball Squad.

Peirce School students began to field unofficial sports teams at the turn of the century, although not as part of a school-sponsored athletic program. Nevertheless, students, faculty, and alumni enjoyed attending the frequently boisterous intercollegiate Y.M.C.A. meetings, held at Association Hall. The Peirce contingent at these meetings was always very vocal, chanting some of "their well known yells:"

Rip, Rap, Rah!
Zip, Zap, Zee!
P-E-I-R-C-E.

Gee whiz!
We mean biz!
Who do?
We do!
Peirce.

College League basketball championship in 1928. The following year, the school fielded its first football team.

In 1930, perhaps motivated by the success of Bill Tilden, world tennis star and Peirce graduate, Peirce School expanded its athletic program to include intercollegiate teams in that sport.

The 1920s produced many glamorous sports heroes. International tennis champion Bill Tilden (left), called by some "the Babe Ruth of tennis," was a Peirce graduate. The 1921 U.S. tennis finals pitted Tilden against Wallace F. Johnson, also a Peirce School alumnus. Above: Peirce School Tennis Team, circa 1930.

Marion Frank (left) led the 1938-1939 Peirce School women's basketball team (below).

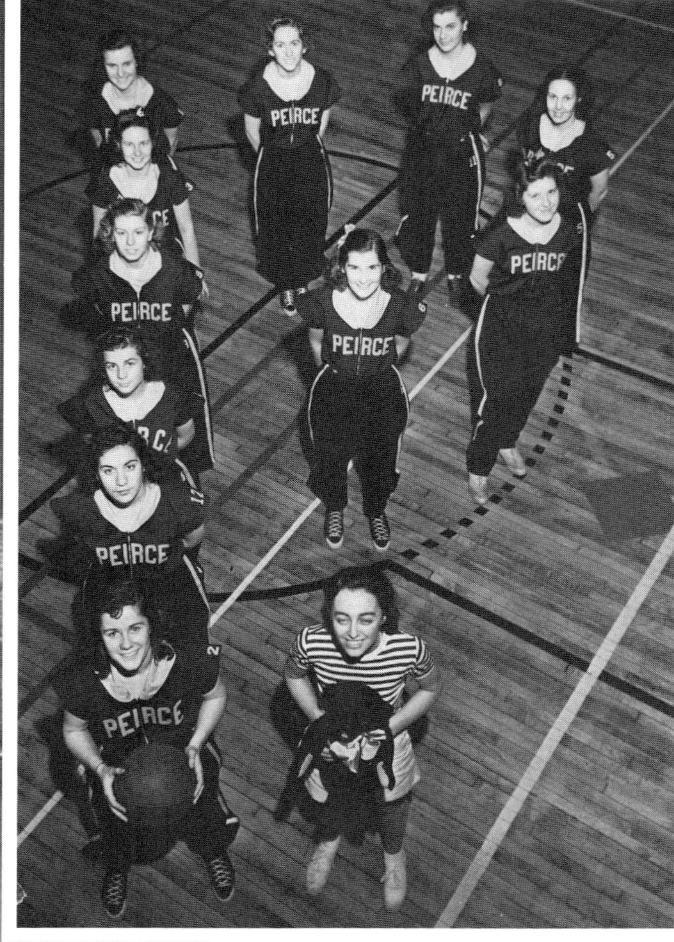

In the 1920s, Peirce's leadership in the field of business education in Philadelphia was unmistakable and unquestioned. By the end of the decade, the Peirce Placement Bureau averaged 2500 applications for graduates yearly. Its business-oriented radio shows were among the most popular of any type in the city. But perhaps the greatest testament to the success of any school is the success of its alumni. In the 1927 edition of Who's Who in Philadelphia, 70% of the businessmen included were either Peirce graduates themselves, or employed Peirce graduates as upper-level executives in their organizations.

One well-chronicled incident from that era illustrates the impeccable reputation enjoyed by Peirce School. Around that time, Leopold Stokowski, director of the Philadelphia Orchestra, was known for his eccentricity and imperious personal demeanor. At one point, Stokowski desired to hire two new secretaries, and he applied in person to Peirce School. After making "his usual semi-royal entrance," Stokowski listed the specific qualifications he expected in his secretaries. Each applicant must have a thorough knowledge of music history. One must speak and write French, the other German; preferably each applicant would understand both languages. One must play violin, the other piano. Furthermore, both must know shorthand, as well as the spellings of technical words and phrases used routinely in the "czar's" correspondence.

Without missing a beat, the Peirce Employment Office Director consulted his files, and calmly recommended two graduates of the Secretarial Division who perfectly met Stokowski's requirements.

In the Coolidge era, "The business of America [was] business." These Peirce ads from the 1920s reflect the upbeat, ambitious sentiment of the times.

Peirce School began another round of academic restructuring in 1930, concentrating this time on its secretarial programs. In that year, the school announced the establishment of a fourth college-grade course, the Executive Secretary Course, which was designed to prepare students entering the business world in entry-level secretarial positions more rapid advancement to executive rank. The course combined elements of the Business Administration and Secretarial programs. This effort continued through 1933, when a Secretarial Administration course was established. The strengthening of the Secretarial Division was designed to offer a "college grade" complement to the Business Administration course.

Two Years Nearer to Your Business Success

If you are considering a college course in Business Administration or Accounting—if you are seeking knowledge without loss of time—this message is of vital importance to you.

If you are unable to devote four years to college, or have found college enrollments filled, we invite you to talk with us regarding the Business Administration Course given at the Peirce School.

It is of university grade, and, although it may be completed in two years, it contains as many credit hours of instruction as the usual four-year course, and in breadth and thoroughness is comparable only to similar courses offered by the larger universities.

An earnest student to whom time and expense is an object may thus cover in two years a course which is ordinarily spread over four years, and thus save two of the most valuable years of his life.

Ask any successful business man or banker what he thinks of Peirce School. Your whole future may depend upon the action you take now.

Other Courses: Executive - Secretary, Accounting, Stenographic-Secretary, 1-year Business. 60th Year Book. Call or write.

PEIRCE SCHOOL
of Business Administration

Pine Street, west of Broad, Philadelphia

By 1935, Peirce School had undergone an extensive fifteen-year cycle of change and refinement in its curricula that successfully adapted the school to changing social, economic, and educational conditions of the early 20th century. The business world had changed dramatically during that period. Scientific management and mass production techniques pioneered by Henry Ford revolutionized thought on industrial organization. One result of the new thinking was the conclusive rise to prominence and rapid numerical expansion of a new breed of business professional, the manager.

This period was also one which saw the maturation of the concept of industrial or vocational education, of which business schools like Peirce were a part. Industrial education had grown to be accepted by the end of the 19th century with the establishment and prosperity of hundreds of schools dedicated, like Peirce, to the transmission of practical, work-related skills. By this time as well, many academic colleges and universities offered programs in engineering, business, finance, and other industrial disciplines. Like the medical and legal professions in the 1870s and 1880s, by the 1920s, many of the occupations peculiar to industry, notably engineering and accounting, had organized and standardized the practice of their crafts, and assumed a professional status of their own. The success of these groups was reflected in the increasing numbers of degree programs established by four-year colleges and universities in these disciplines.

By 1935, the curricular restructuring of the past fifteen years left Peirce School firmly in line with modern developments, and enabled it to compete successfully in the modern era. The reorganization left

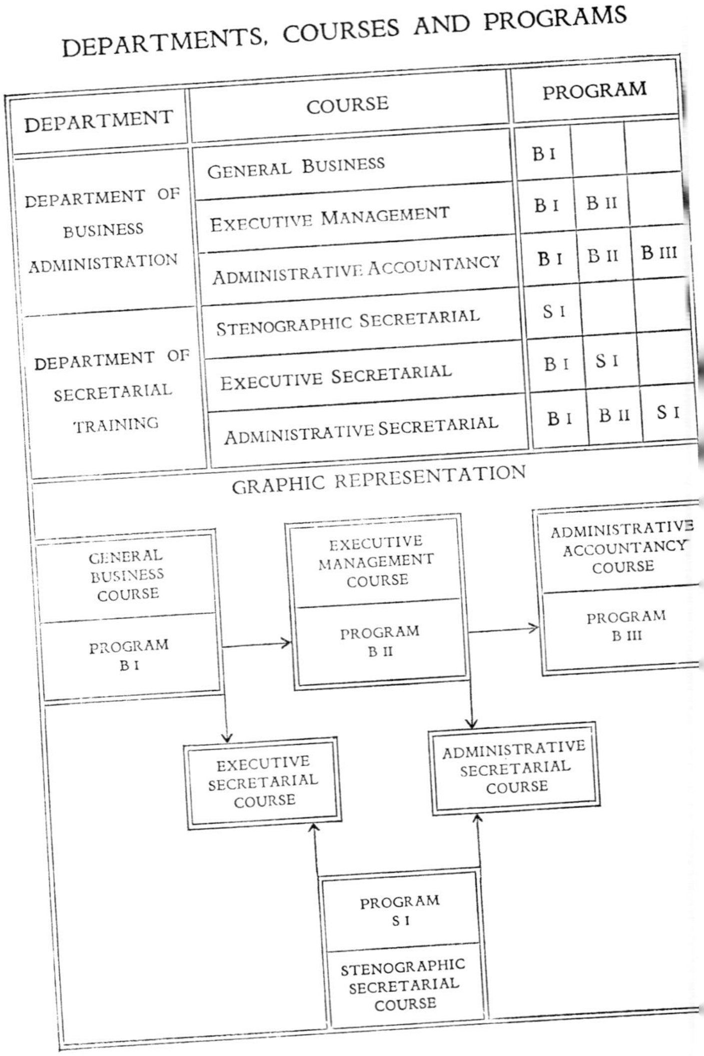

DEPARTMENTS, COURSES AND PROGRAMS

DEPARTMENT	COURSE	PROGRAM		
DEPARTMENT OF BUSINESS ADMINISTRATION	GENERAL BUSINESS	B I		
	EXECUTIVE MANAGEMENT	B I	B II	
	ADMINISTRATIVE ACCOUNTANCY	B I	B II	B III
DEPARTMENT OF SECRETARIAL TRAINING	STENOGRAPHIC SECRETARIAL	S I		
	EXECUTIVE SECRETARIAL	B I	S I	
	ADMINISTRATIVE SECRETARIAL	B I	B II	S I

GRAPHIC REPRESENTATION

GENERAL BUSINESS COURSE
PROGRAM B I
EXECUTIVE MANAGEMENT COURSE
PROGRAM B II
ADMINISTRATIVE ACCOUNTANCY COURSE
PROGRAM B III
EXECUTIVE SECRETARIAL COURSE
ADMINISTRATIVE SECRETARIAL COURSE
PROGRAM S I
STENOGRAPHIC SECRETARIAL COURSE

This complex chart, reproduced from the 1937-1938 Peirce School catalog, depicts a closely interlocking curriculum, the result of over fifteen years of academic restructuring.

SUBJECTS OF STUDY AND PROGRAMS

SUBJECTS	PROGRAMS				
	SECRETARIAL TRAINING		BUSINESS ADMINISTRATION		
R Indicates Required E Indicates Elective	CODES	S I	B I	B II	B III
ACCOUNTING AND AUDITING	A			R	R
BOOKKEEPING AND RECORDS	A	E	R		
CREDITS AND COLLECTIONS	Ec			R	
ECONOMICS — GEOGRAPHY	Ec		R		
ECONOMICS, CONTEMPORARY	Ec			R	R
ENGLISH — WORD STUDY	E	R	R		
ENGLISH — CONSTRUCTION	E	R	R		
ENGLISH — COMPOSITION	E	R	R	R	R
ETHICS, THE PRINCIPLES OF	So	R	R	R	R
FILING & INDEX SYSTEMS	O	R			
FOREIGN LANGUAGE STUDY	F	E	E	E	E
GRAPHS AND CHARTS	Ec			R	
INSURANCE, GENERAL & LIFE	Ec			R	
INVESTMENTS — SECURITIES	Ec			R	R
LAW AND LEGAL FORMS	L		R	R	R
MACHINE CALCULATION	M	E	R	R	R
MANAGEMENT, INDUSTRIAL	Ec			R	
MANAGEMENT, OFFICE	Ec			R	
MANAGEMENT, PERSONNEL	Ec			R	
MATHEMATICS: ARITHMETIC	M	E	R	R	R
MONEY, BANKING & FINANCE	Ec		R	R	
OFFICE APPLIANCES, ETC.	O	R	R		
OFFICE PRACTICE & DUTIES	O	R			
ORGANIZATION, FINANCING	Ec			R	R
PENMANSHIP, HANDWRITING	P	R	R	E	E
PSYCHOLOGY — PRACTICAL	So	E	E	R	R
SALES AND DISTRIBUTION	Sa			R	
SHORTHAND: GREGG, PITMAN	S	R			
TAXES—FEDERAL & STATE	A			R	R
TYPEWRITING TECHNIQUE	T	R	R	E	E

Peirce with three major educational divisions: the Departments of Business Administration and Secretarial Training in the day school, and the Department of Specialized Training in the evening school. Each division of the day school offered three options, ranging in sophistication and length of from one to three years.

The foundation of the offerings of the Business Administration department remained the one-year general business course. As in Thomas May Peirce's time, the business administration courses progressed from theory of accounts, arithmetic, penmanship, English, and more modern financial and commercial subjects to simulated experience in the Banking and Business Department.

The two-year Executive Management course built upon the core of the General Business course, adding a second year of theoretical and practical study of such topics as economics, insurance, management, accounting, salesmanship, and sociology. The three-year Administrative Accountancy program combined the entire general business and executive management courses with advanced accounting topics leading to qualification for the C.P.A. exam.

A similarly interlocking curricular format obtained in the Secretarial Training department. Offerings progressed in yearly increments from the basic, one-year Stenographic Secretarial course, which offered proficiency in shorthand and typewriting as well as fundamentals of accounting, English, and office practice. The two-year Executive Secretarial program combined the General Business course with the Stenographic Secretarial, and the Administrative Secretarial program combined General Business, Executive Management, and Stenographic Secretarial courses into a three-year program.

The Department of Specialized Training in the evening school offered shorter, specifically vocational courses in addition to all the day programs. Some of the special courses included Real Estate and Conveyencing, Machine Calculation, Sales and Distribution, preparation for the Civil Service examination, and advanced courses in business topics geared for students and graduates of commercial high schools.

In 1934, Thomas May Peirce, Jr., C.P.A. (1878-1945), joined his half-sister Mary Peirce in the management of the school. Peirce assumed the office of Administrative Executive, which he would hold until his death in 1945. Peirce, a graduate of the Central Manual Training School of Philadelphia and the University of Pennsylvania, served in the 2nd Pennsylvania Regiment during the Spanish-American War, and received a diploma in Shorthand and Typewriting from Peirce School in 1899. Prior to this time, Peirce had operated a successful accounting firm in the city.

The range of student activities at Peirce continued to expand through the 1930s. In 1931, Sigma Gamma Omega, a brotherhood of professional accountants, became the first fraternity to operate at Peirce when it established a Pennsylvania Alpha chapter at the school. Three years later, an elective Student Council was created to "meet at periodic intervals to discuss matters of mutual interest to student and instructor." Disputes referred to the Student Council concerned such issues as "discipline, holiday periods and work assignments." In addition to athletics, fraternities, and student government, the school also sponsored a Choral Society, School Orchestra, Dramatic club, and Debating Society, as well as a Journalism club that published two school newspapers, the short-lived Peircentinel and the ubiquitous Peircetonian. Other social activities included a series of Friday afternoon teas sponsored by Mary Peirce, dances, and horsemanship classes.

Facing page: The Peirce School Brains Trust, 1938. Left to right: Thomas May Peirce, Jr., Mary B. Peirce, Thomas May Peirce III, and Ruth Peirce Taylor. The range of social activities on campus expanded through the 1930s. Right: a fraternity pledge, circa 1940. Below: Mary B. Peirce (seated, center) hosts the Peirce School Choral Society at the family residence, 1616 North Broad Street, in 1940.

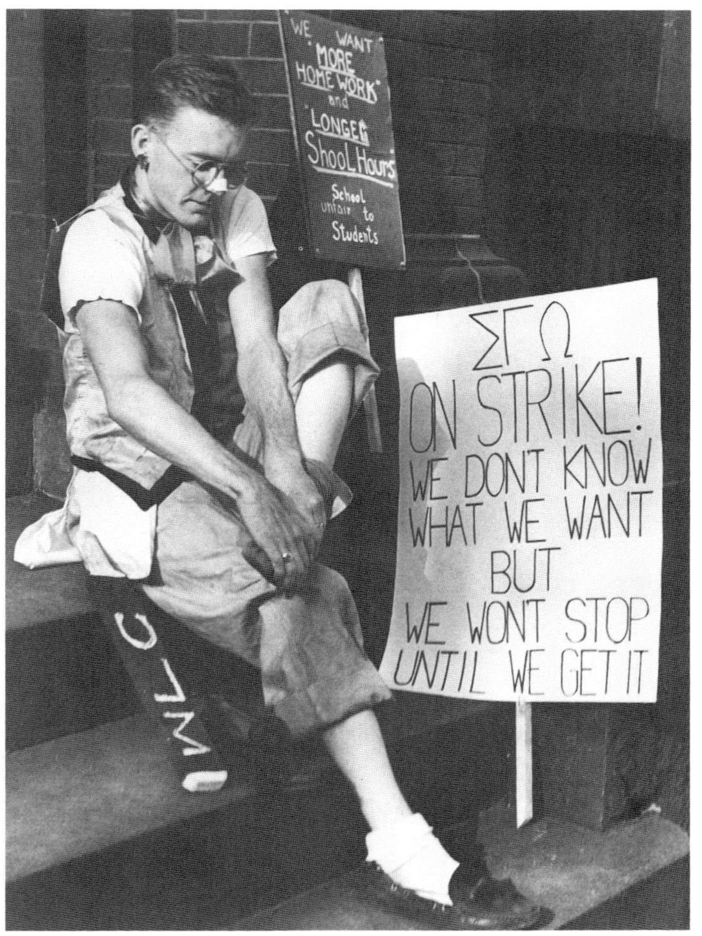

WE WANT
MORE
HOME WORK"
and
LONGER
ShooL Hours
School
unfair to
Students
ΣΓΩ
ON STRIKE!
WE DONT KNOW
WHAT WE WANT
BUT
WE WONT STOP
UNTIL WE GET IT

In 1939, Handel and Haydn Hall, the original home of the Union Business College, was demolished. Although architectural alterations over the years had changed the face of the old music hall considerably, it still outlasted two later sites of the school, the Inman and Record Buildings. The Hall enjoyed popularity in the latter decades of the 19th century until the Reading Railroad moved its terminal from Ninth and Green to Tenth and Market in 1893. In 1906, the building was sold, to be renovated for factory purposes.

With American entry into World War II, Peirce School once again prided itself on preparing both civilian and government workers to contribute efficiently to the bureaucratic operations of the modern military. Peirce School resisted the practice, followed by many other institutions during the early years of the war, to "accelerate" course work to improve the flow of young men and women into the armed forces and other vital war-related positions. The school reasoned that its programs were already shorter than most, and that shortening courses would inevitably lead to ill-prepared, and therefore inefficient workers. As in all other schools, the war caused a sharp drop in attendance at Peirce. At one point, only two of seven floors were needed for class and administration at the Peirce School building.

As World War II drew to a close, Peirce School suffered the loss of Thomas May Peirce, Jr., who died in 1945. As America entered the post-war era, with an increasingly degree-conscious society and competitive educational community, capable and energetic leadership would play a crucial role in the school's attempt to adapt to the demands of the future.

Disparate Depression-Era Images at Peirce School. Above, right: a chilly cigarette break on the school steps; (right) sunny "Peirce girls" in the "Flowers for the Flowerless" parade, flanking the school limousine, in 1938. Facing page, top: Thomas May Peirce, Jr., Mary B. Peirce, and John A. Luman visit a school office in 1941.

In 1939, Peirce School acquired 1426 Pine Street, the property directly adjoining the main school building (visible in photo at left). At one time, the house had been occupied by Dr. Horace Howard Furness, a noted Shakespearian scholar. Dr. Furness was the brother of architect Frank Furness, who designed many famous Philadelphia buildings of the era, including the Broad Street Station, the Pennsylvania Academy of Fine Arts, and the Library of the University of Pennsylvania.

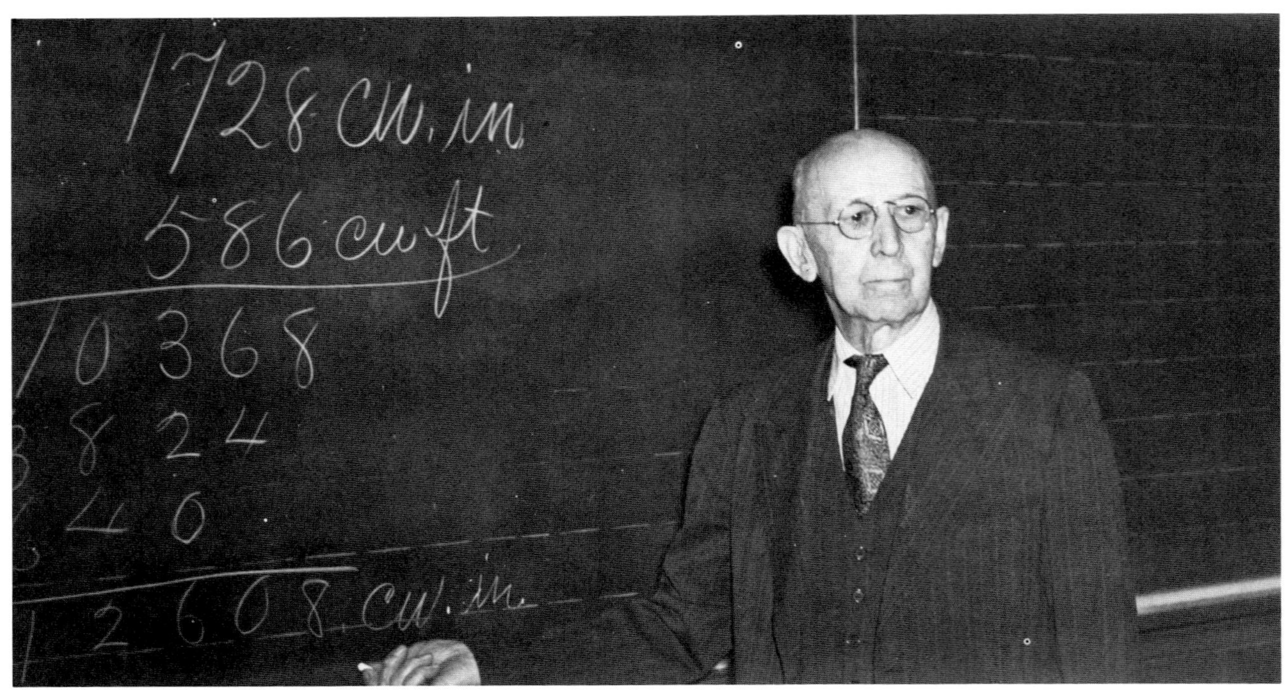

Above: E. J. Conner, instructor in commercial arithmetic, makes a point to his class, circa 1947. Right: Members of the Peirce School staff welcome Nicaraguan President and Peirce Alumnus, Anastasio Somoza (third from left) in 1939.

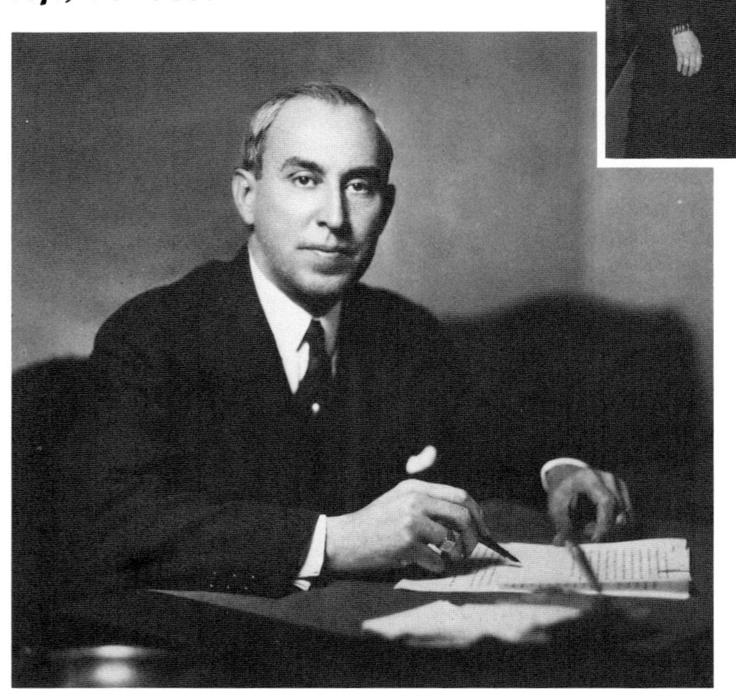

Left: Another graduate of the Latin-American Department, Andres Pastoriza, Minister to the United States from the Dominican Republic, 1938.

Longevity at Peirce. Left: William Raymond Thorne, 1916 Peirce graduate, and administrator at the school for nearly 45 years. Below: Ann Bennett Peirce, alumna, teacher, and daughter of Thomas May Peirce, Jr. Below right: Professor Samuel N. Talman, who taught at Peirce for 44 years, from 1898 to 1942. Bottom: Sarah M. Hoy tends the cafeteria cash register, circa 1923. She served until about 1950.

Thomas May Peirce III assumed the desk of Chief Executive Officer of Peirce School in 1946.

Chapter 5
Peirce School Becomes Peirce Junior College

In 1946, Thomas May Peirce III joined Peirce School of Business Administration as "Managing Partner, Chief Executive Officer." Peirce graduated from Dartmouth College in 1926 and Peirce School four years later, and served as president of the Peirce School Alumni Association in 1937 and 1938. Peirce interrupted a career with Central Penn National Bank to serve in the Supply Corps of the United States Naval Reserve throughout World War II, rising to the rank of Lieutenant Commander.

With these credentials, Peirce possessed a solid business and administrative background. An incident from his early career serves to illustrate a commensurate boldness and tenacity. In 1930, a young Thomas May Peirce III finished his schooling. With the Depression gripping the nation and limiting employment opportunities, Peirce decided to fulfill a life-long ambition to go to sea and see the world. Peirce decided to approach the matter directly. With a like-minded former Dartmouth classmate, Peirce walked to the apex of the Benjamin Franklin Bridge, then less than five years old, and watched downriver for a merchant vessel to come in. Spotting one, the young men waited for it to berth, counted the piers to the ship from the base of the bridge, and ran down to find it. Clambering up the rope ladder, Peirce and his friend located the ship's captain and managed to obtain seaman's jobs on a ship departing New York the following week.

Arriving at an East River pier on the appointed day, the men were outraged to find that an executive with the shipping firm had filled the openings with two applicants of his own choosing. Rather than accept the situation, Peirce and his friend went directly to the executive offices of the line, dumped their duffels on the floor, and announced they would not leave without seeing the vice president in question. After a lengthy delay, during which their resolve remained unshaken, Peirce and his friend obtained places on another ship.

Peirce brought this same determination and boldness to the executive offices of Peirce School. When he arrived in 1946, the school, in his own words, was "flat on its back." World War II, following hard on the heels of the Depression, had reduced the once-proud school to a shadow of its former self. By 1945, enrollment had dropped to 200. Mortgage payments languished overdue. Without immediate attention, Peirce School was in danger of collapse.

Peirce School was not alone in suffering enrollment slippage during the war, when the armed forces siphoned off the lion's share of the college-age population. The school's problems, however, ran even deeper than that, and had their roots in the Great Depression. Widespread economic pressures hurt enrollment in a number of ways. Fewer potential students possessed the financial means to attend school. Depressed business activity diminished employment opportunities that had served to lure students to Peirce School in the past. Moreover, and perhaps most significantly in the long term, the Depression helped change public attitudes toward careers in business. Greed and excess by big business was seen by many as a prime cause of the nation's troubles. The image of the businessman, revered nearly as a national icon as recently as the 1920s, had been deeply tarnished by public distrust. In this light, the war-related enrollment problems only heightened a disturbing trend.

Thomas May Peirce's first priority in reviving the school was to hire a professional educator to serve as Dean. Shortly after his arrival, Peirce found just the man he was looking for in William J. Hamilton. Hamilton, who possessed an impressive background in commercial education, became Dean of the School in October, 1946.

Thomas May Peirce III confers with Dean William J. Hamilton, circa 1946.

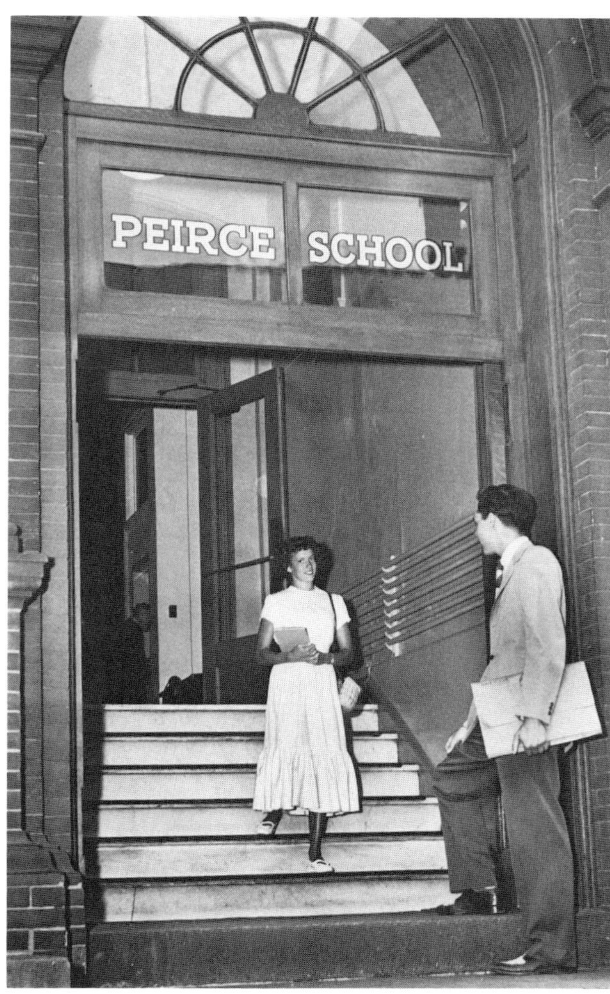

Above: Social life in the post-war era. Below: A student at work on a modern business machine, circa 1948.

The end of World War II provided a temporary respite to these concerns, as tens of thousand of returning veterans attended American colleges on the GI Bill. Peirce School shared in this bonanza, and quickly reversed its fortunes in the post-war years. However, Thomas May Peirce realized that underlying, fundamental problems must be addressed if the school's prosperity was to be sustained in the coming decades.

The curriculum established at Peirce School between 1920-1935 carried the school, with only minor alterations, to the dawn of the 1950s. Peirce recognized that business, and especially educational methods, had evolved dramatically since the last cycle of change undergone at the school in the 1920s and 1930s. World War II, had produced a wealth of technological change and promised to usher in a world of previously unimagined complexity. Atomic energy, jet and rocket propulsion, and increasing Cold War tensions brought phrases like "the education gap" to the public discourse. Functioning in this new, highly technical "space age" society, Peirce and others realized, would require a college education. Enrollment in engineering and other technologically-based disciplines increased sharply. The enormous numbers of World War II veterans attending college on the GI Bill seemed to foreshadow this trend. Moreover, as the 1950s progressed, demographic projections indicated that the numbers of college-age population would rise rapidly during the 1960s. Taking these and other factors into account, Thomas May Peirce III set a program of modernization in motion at Peirce School that would ensure its viability in the coming decades.

One of Peirce's goals was to continually improve the school's academic standing. In 1948, Peirce School became one of only ten schools in the country to be granted membership in Business Education Associates [later Business Education Research Associates], a non-profit organization "devoted to the improvement of standards in business education."

Throughout the early 1950s, Peirce initiated a number of specialized certificate programs within its secretarial department, including such "growing" occupations as medical and airline secretary, and medical and office receptionist. One significant innovation in this period was the introduction of a Practical Business Department in the Secretarial Division. This department consisted of a model office where, as in its older counterpart in the Business Administration department, secretarial students progressed through a hierarchy of positions, refining skills in a simulated office environment.

In an administrative reorganization in late 1951, Thomas May Peirce III was appointed President and Treasurer of Peirce School of Business Administration following its incorporation. President Peirce brought tireless energy and dynamism to

Thomas May Peirce III blended innovation with tradition to revive a flagging Peirce School in the post-World War II years. Above: a field trip for the new Airline Secretarial course; (facing page) the Merchants Commercial Company, successor to the original Thomas M. Peirce & Company in the Banking and Business Department.

the school's administration. In consistency with his naval background, Peirce ran a tight ship. His contemporaries recalled that it was not unusual for him to work three or four days at the school almost without interruption. These marathon sessions often included midnight tours of the building, accompanied only by a security guard, that inevitably resulted in mountains of memos on administrative desks the following morning. President Peirce quickly gained respect for his efficiency, dedication, and attention to detail.

President Peirce also displayed foresight and an ability to adapt to the times. In 1953, Peirce became one of the first schools to be accredited as a "Junior College of Business" by the newly organized Accrediting Commission for Business Schools in Washington, D.C. The ACBS had attained the approval of the U.S. Office of Education. The change, which allowed Peirce School students greater freedom in transferring credit for course work to other institutions, forced Peirce School into conformity with modern educational standards. A formalized credit system was adopted for the first time. The traditional individual progress system, in effect for 88 years, was finally abandoned. By the late 1950s, the practical Banking and Business Department, for many years one of the most prominent features of Peirce School, was reluctantly phased into other programs.

In 1959, Peirce School's Office Automation Division opened, offering courses in computer operation and data processing. In keeping with Peirce's tradition for innovation in business education, this was reputed to be the "first Business Data Processing educational program in the Eastern United States." For the first few years, the content of the program was administered by Automation Institute of America with Peirce as its franchisee in the Philadelphia area. The program included fundamentals of computer technology and programming, and thorough grounding in the operation of the card punch data entry method.

By 1960, the time of the death of Mary B. Peirce, over 150,000 students had attended the school since 1865. 20,000 graduates, roughly two-thirds of them women, had obtained diplomas at Peirce. Student activities had grown to embrace two new Greek societies, Pi Sigma Chi fraternity for marketing and management students, and Pi Sigma Alpha, a sorority of secretarial students. Other student organizations, in addition to those already mentioned, included the Foreign Student Club, the Press Club, the Receptionist Club. In addition, Peirce students sponsored and organized an annual fashion show.

Peirce School in Transition. A secretarial student (above) learns elements of poise and bearing in a "finishing" course, while (below) business automation students study computer technology.

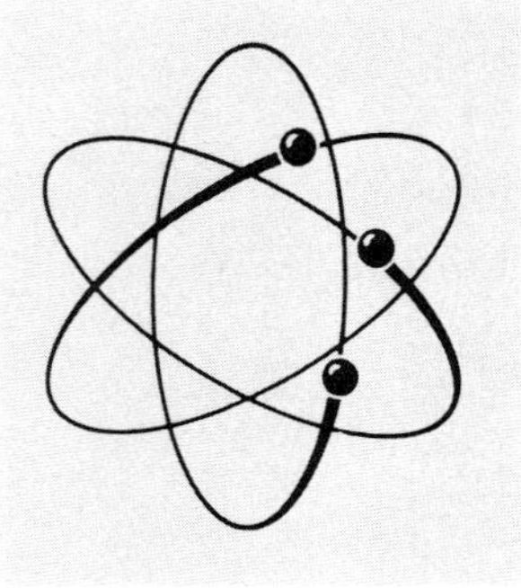

These illustrations from the 1961 school catalog show career opportunities for women.

* Put yourself in this picture—with the help of Peirce School. American business provides unlimited opportunities for well-trained men and women to earn good salaries while enjoying interesting and varied careers.

Peirce Junior College

President Peirce realized the difficulties that the modern era posed to a proprietary institution such as Peirce School. Keen competition and spiraling costs had forced many such schools to close their doors. In 1963, after 98 years as a proprietary institution, Peirce petitioned the Philadelphia Court of Common Pleas to change the status of the Peirce School of Business Administration corporation from profit to non-profit, to be operated by a nine-member Board of Trustees. The first board consisted of Harrison F. Dunning, president of Scott Paper Company; Dr. Karl R. Friedmann, Sc.D., president of Girard College, Earl G. Glazier, president and director of Hardwick and Magee Company; Morris H. Goldman, Esq., member of the law firm Wolf, Block, Schorr, and Solis-Cohen; Dr. William J. Hamilton, vice-president and dean of Peirce School; Dr. Kenneth G. Matheson, dean of faculty at Drexel Institute; Casimir A. Sienkiewicz, chairman of the board and chief executive of Central-Penn National Bank; John Rodman Wanamaker, chairman of the board of John Wanamaker of Philadelphia; and President Thomas May Peirce III.

1.

2.

3.

4.

5.

6.

The First Peirce Junior College Board of Trustees. 1.) John Rodman Wanamaker, 2.) Earl W. Glazier, 3.) Thomas May Peirce III, 4.) William J. Hamilton, 5.) Morris H. Goldman, 6.) Kenneth G. Matheson, 7.) Karl R. Friedman, 8.) Harrison F. Dunning, and 9.) Casimir A. Sienkiewicz.

9.

7.

8.

THE PEIRCETONIAN

OL. XXVII No. 4 PHILADELPHIA, PA. JUNE, 19

Hail! Peirce Junior College!

E SCHOOL BECOMES JUNIOR COLLEGE

there's a new career for you in business

automation

A NEW FIELD WHICH CAN MEAN MORE MONEY, A BETTER JOB FOR YOU

AUTOMATION INSTITUTE COURSES

OFFICE AUTOMATION DIVISION PEIRCE School of Business Administration 1420 Pine Street PEnnypacker 5-2100

A banner headline welcomes Peirce Junior College. Below: The Computer Center, 1622 Chestnut Street, 1965.

In 1964, as the school opened its centennial year, Peirce School of Business Administration received approval from Commonwealth of Pennsylvania to grant associate degrees in both arts and sciences and operate as a junior college. Peirce Junior College, in addition to its Business Administration and Secretarial divisions, created a Liberal Arts division that enabled its graduates to transfer credits to four-year colleges and universities. The school retained its traditional certificate programs in General Business, Stenography, Secretarial Finishing, and Office Automation to accommodate students interested only in achieving certification in specific business skills.

As Peirce Junior College, the school continued its tradition of innovative and progressive vocational education. In 1965, the school opened a second center city branch at 1622 Chestnut Street to house its Automation Division. Known as the Computer Center, this second-floor location housed five classrooms, computer laboratory and keypunch machine rooms, as well as faculty office and conference space. Computer students split class time between the Center and the Pine Street building.

An exhaustive seven-year period of self-evaluation culminated in the achievement of accreditation by the independent Middle States Association of Colleges and Secondary Schools in 1971. The approval by an independent agency such a Middle States is an important aspect of modern college operation. It carries prestige and the support of other member institutions, as well as eligibility for government funding. Most important, however, accreditation permits Peirce Junior College students full transfer of credits to four-year colleges and universities.

Accreditation is an exhaustive process, and Peirce took this step in careful increments. Between 1964 and 1968, Peirce Junior College held "correspondent" status, which allowed it to utilize approved Middle States consultants to prepare for admission. As part of this process, the college built a new enlarged library on the seventh floor.

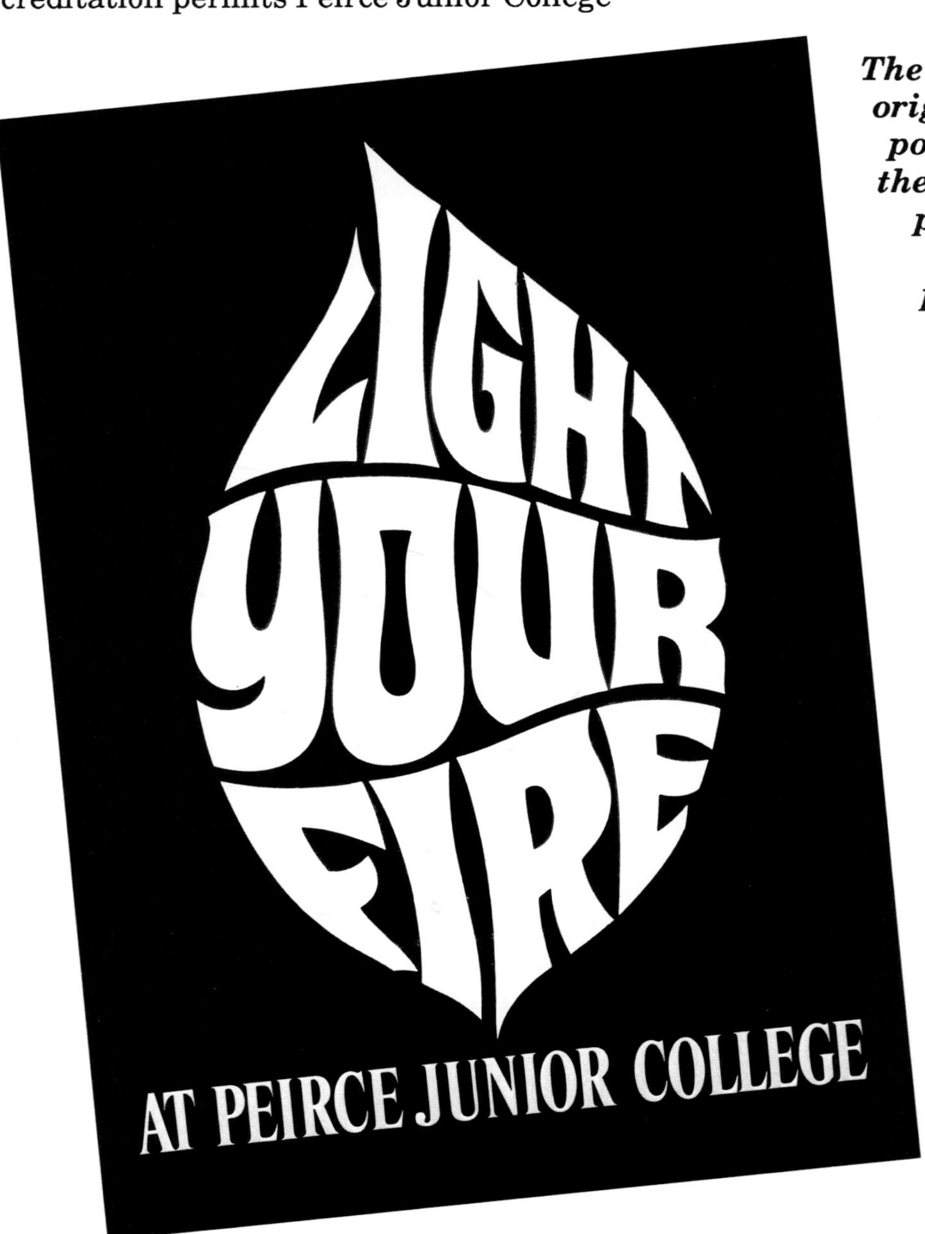

The flaming colors of the original 1968 recruiting poster (left) symbolized the intense activity that preceded regional accreditation. Facing page: By 1967, a modern college library stood on the girders of the old, seventh-floor running track.

On the strength of this and other improvements, Peirce achieved "candidate" status in 1968. For a period of sixteen months, the school bent to the task of preparing a comprehensive self-evaluation and formal application, only to have it rejected in April, 1970. Middle States requirements were stringent, and mandated further improvement in several aspects of the school's operation. Finally, in December, 1971, the Middle States Association of Colleges and Secondary Schools accepted Peirce Junior College as a member institution.

Overall enrollment approached 2000 by the late 1960s, a testament not only to the success of Thomas May Peirce's programs and leadership, but to the coming of age of the post-World War II "baby boom" generation. With many businesses and this new generation of students located increasingly outside the center of Philadelphia, Peirce began to consider adding a suburban campus to complement its urban location. In 1969, the college acquired the seventy-five acre Patterson estate in Devon, Pennsylvania. Although the school also considered a site in Valley Forge, the Devon location was considered ideal. The college formulated a six-year plan that would culminate, if all went well, in a largely residential student body of 600 by 1975.

Unfortunately, little went well with the Devon plan. Local residents opposed the plan from the start, erecting zoning barriers which blocked renovation of the site. After a six-year battle, which included false starts and acrimony in alternation, Peirce reluctantly abandoned the plan. The bitter taste of the Devon experience lingered, effectively scuttling later expansion hopes almost as soon as they surfaced, including a potential move to Exton in 1987.

Despite the Devon disappointment, President Peirce continued refinement and expansion of the school's curricula through the 1970s. Before his retirement in 1981, the school established Retail and Fashion Merchandising programs, a Data Processing Secretarial Program, which merged traditional secretarial with computer skills, an International Business and Secretarial program, and a Hospitality Management program. One of Peirce's more successful innovations in this period was the establishment of a Court Reporting program in 1975. This course, the only one of its kind in the eastern United States to be approved by the National Shorthand Reporters Association at the time of its inception, has maintained critical and popular acclaim.

Dr. Raymond C. Lewin replaced the retiring Thomas May Peirce III as president in 1981. Dr. Lewin became the first chief administrator of the school not to bear the Peirce name, but nevertheless continued the line of capable Peirce administrators. Dr. Lewin obtained his Ed.D. from Columbia University, and held experience in educational administration at Montclair State College and Fairleigh Dickinson University, where he was Dean of the Edward Williams College.

Dr. Lewin brought a different approach to Peirce, one which manifested itself almost immediately. In 1983, the college acquired title to the Pine Street building from the Peirce family. Ownership of the building allowed Dr. Lewin to move ahead with financing for major renovations and face-lifting to the aging physical plant.

Less tangibly, however, Dr. Lewin's commitment to a personal style of democratic management contrasted sharply with the management-by-command model that had characterized managerial thought

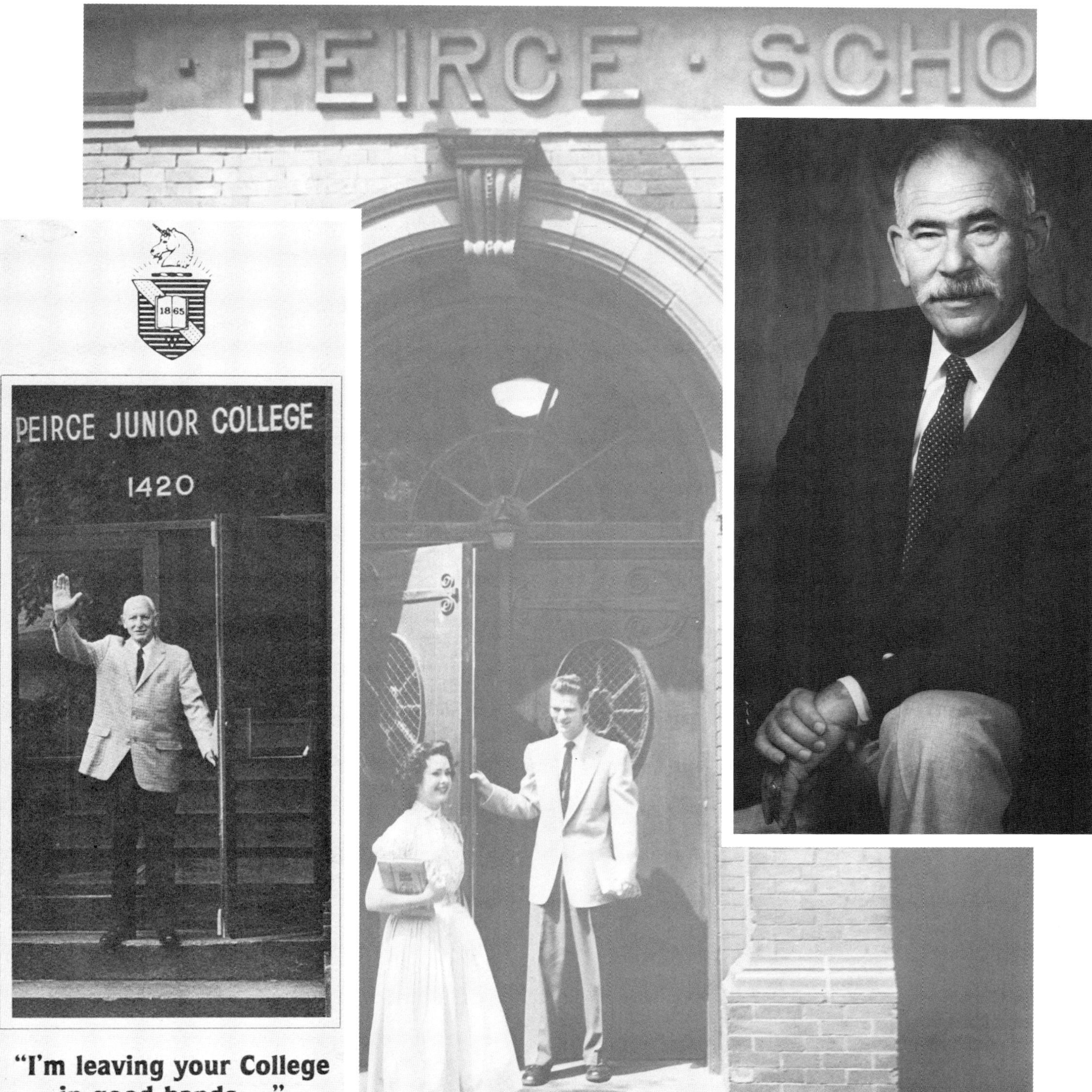

"I'm leaving your College in good hands..."

Dr Raymond C. Lewin assumed the office of president in 1981 after the retirement of Thomas May Peirce III

in previous generations. Dr. Lewin broadened the size and responsibility of Administrative Council and delegated as much authority as possible. In addition, he increased formal contractual commitment to capable faculty and staff. The result has been increased communication and involvement in college operation, an environment which breeds initiative and encourages excellence.

PEIRCE
SCHOOL
PEIRCE
SCHOOL
PEIRC
SCHOO

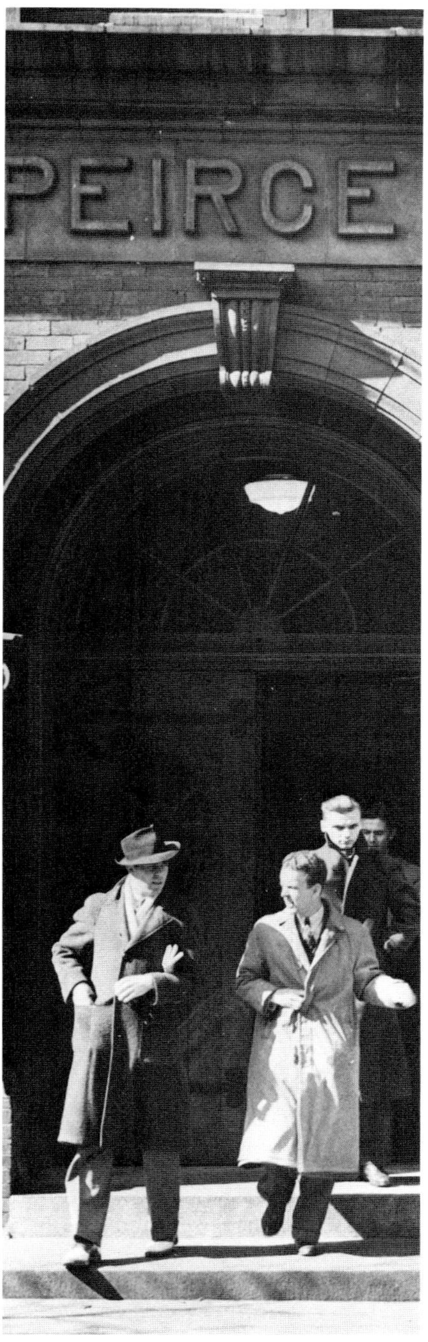

A recurrent theme in Peirce memorabilia was the doorway of the school as a visual metaphor of the doorway to success. These photos of students in passage, from six different eras, reflect that concept.

PROOF

The Saturday Evening Post
Philadelphia

June 27 — 168 lines
$252.

Paid 6/22/08

252.
12.60
239.40

Also paid for cut $28.50

Each of These Men Has Praised the Methods and the Work of

Peirce School
Philadelphia

Each loomed large in his day. All have been the men "in the firm"—partners with Uncle Sam in the biggest, grandest country in the world.

When a young man is "admitted to the firm," he experiences his first sense of proprietorship. He is working for himself—he has gained the end toward which he has been striving.

Business is never a closed corporation. Firms the world over are waiting for the young man who proves that he is worthy of the trust. America is reaching out to-day for young men who are to be "partners" in her commercial supremacy.

Ask yourself this question: "Am I prepared to fill the post when the opportunity presents itself?"

Peirce School Prepares Young Men and Women for Positions of Trust in Business

It is America's foremost business school. The course of study combines a general education with a technical training in commercial subjects. Its classes are carefully graded and are adapted to graduates of colleges and preparatory schools, as well as to those who have had but a grammar-school education. The course of study requires from six months to two years for its completion, depending upon the qualifications and ability of the student. Boarding-students are received under the personal care of the Director.

Peirce School Develops Initiative

Peirce graduates may be found all over the world in positions of trust and responsibility. They will be found at every cross-roads of business where initiative is ~~demanded~~ required — the demand for Peirce graduates far exceeds the supply.

Write for year book, and special literature giving names of successful Peirce graduates.

PEIRCE SCHOOL
Record Building **Philadelphia**
L. B. MOFFETT, Director

13919—52—June 27—¼ page

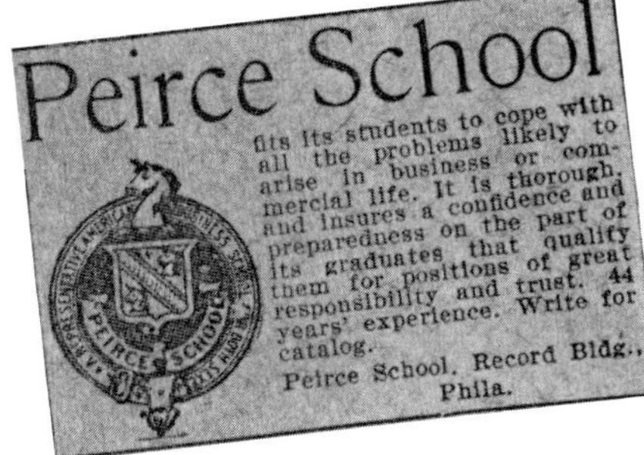

Peirce Junior College draws on a rich heritage as "America's foremost business school" as these advertisements, circa 1908, attest.

President Lewin reinforced Peirce's historical commitment to leadership in business education, establishing computer-related courses and maintaining "state-of-the-art" methods and facilities. Furthermore, the school continued to expand its offerings. The paralegal studies program, established in 1985 with the approval of the American Bar Association, quickly became one of the school's more popular offerings.

Throughout much of its history, Peirce has maintained a position on the cutting edge of vocational education. In 1865, Thomas May Peirce, through the Union Business College, helped to pioneer practical, career-oriented education in Philadelphia and the nation. Thomas May Peirce's foresight and acumen in the fields of education and commerce provided the major impetus which drove the school's continued success. Peirce's vision—in anticipating the growth in commercial professions which accompanied the "Gilded Age" of industrial expansion; in recognizing the potential of women in the public sphere at a time when few, including many women themselves, did so; in recognizing, before many of his contemporaries, the value of practical alternatives to classical higher education—placed Peirce School at the heart of American progress well into the twentieth century.

Peirce School reached the height of its prominence in the 1920s, a visible institutional exponent of contemporary America's most overt cultural ideals. "The business of America is business," said President Coolidge in 1925, giving voice to a national ethic that placed the highest value on business skills. As a leader in American commercial education, Peirce School basked in the spotlight produced by its achievement in the nation's most respected field.

Although Peirce maintained its reputation for offering high quality and innovative programs—adding programs in accounting and strengthening its business and secretarial curriculum—events tempered the position of business education in the national limelight in the twenty years following Coolidge's pronouncement.

The Great Depression, popularly ascribed to commercial greed and excess, tarnished the reputation of the businessman. Moreover, spectacular technological advances during World War II, among them atomic energy and jet propulsion, combined with Cold War tensions to refocus much of American educational attention. Engineering and related technical fields dominated the imaginations of career-minded Americans in the wake of World War II in much the same way as had business in the 1920s.

Thomas May Peirce III successfully adapted Peirce School to the modern era. Peirce maintained the school's vocational orientation. However, following in the innovative tradition established by his grandfather, Peirce broadened the school's curriculum, embracing office technology, related fields of business specialization, and nontraditional business fields such as court reporting. In achieving accredited junior college status, Dr. Peirce adapted the school to rapidly evolving standards of education.

President Peirce's early venture into computers might be seen as a key, correctly anticipating, as did his grandfather in the 1860s, a broad, new field of business professionalization. This decision placed a Peirce business education firmly in the mainstream of high technology, merging, in effect, the two dominant vocational trends of recent generations.

Well over one century after Thomas May Peirce established the Union Business College, its lineal descendent, Peirce Junior College, continues the proud heritage established by its founder. Peirce Junior College owes its continued success not only to the vision and energy of Thomas May Peirce, but also to the many capable and dedicated educators, administrators, and supportive alumni who maintained Dr. Peirce's commitment to innovation and uncompromising excellence over the intervening years. Moreover, the college has maintained its career-oriented ideals. Well into its second century, "Peirce Still Means Business."

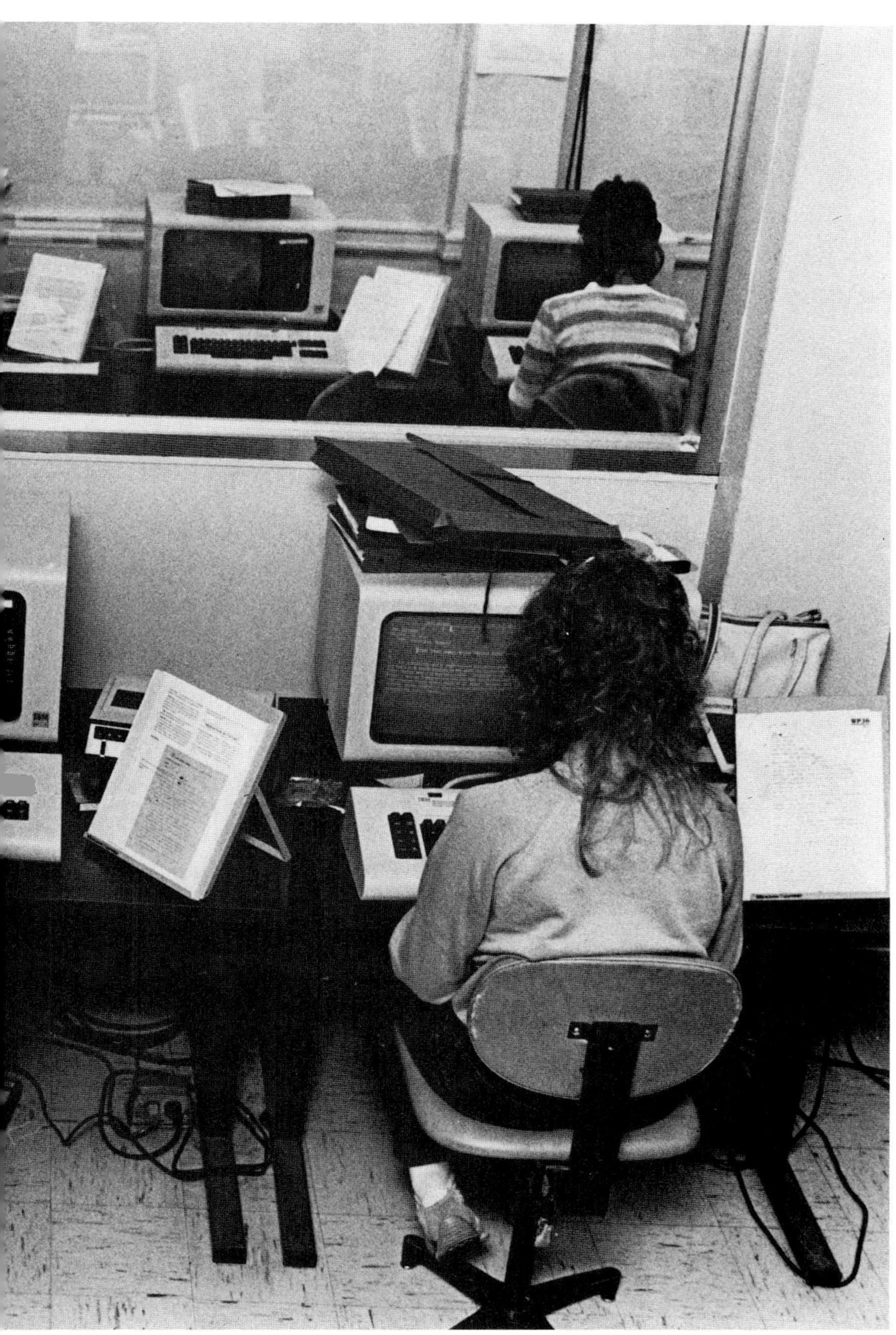

Peirce Junior College
1865 - 1989

PEIRCE MEANS BUSINESS

Appendix A
Peirce Junior College Commencement Speakers 1882--1988

1882	J.M. Buckley, D.D.	Editor, "Christian Advocate"
	Hon. George B. Loring, M.D.	U.S. Commissioner of Education
1883	Bishop Matthew Simpson, DD., LL.D.	M.E. Bishop
	Gen. Clinton B. Fisk	Temperance Advocate
1884	T. DeWitt Talmage, D.D.	Doctor of Divinity
	John Wanamaker	Merchant and Philanthropist
1885	Charles J. Little, Ph.D., LL.D.	President, Northwestern University
	John B. Gough	Temperance Advocate
1886	J.O. Peck, D.D.	Doctor of Divinity
	Chancellor John Hall, D.D., LL.D.	Doctor of Divinity
1887	Samuel W. Small, D.D.	Doctor of Divinity
	Samuel P. Jones	Clergyman and Lecturer
1888	Russell H. Conwell, D.D.	Founder of Temple University
	Robert J. Burdette	Lecturer and Humorist
1889	Bishop Cyrus D. Foss, D.D., LL.D	M.E. Bishop
	George E. Reed, D.D., S.T.D.	President, Dickinson College
1890	Francis L. Patton, D.D., LL.D.	President, Princeton University
	Col. George W. Bain	Lecturer and Journalist
1891	Andrew Carnegie	Industrialist and Philanthropist
	Robert J. Burdette	Lecturer and Humorist
1892	Hon. Edwin S. Stuart	Former Governor of Pennsylvania
	Hon. Chauncey M. Depew, LL.D.	U.S. Senator from New York
1893	Hon. Benjamin Harrison	Former President of the United States
	Frederick Fraley	President, Girard College
1894	Hon. Thomas B. Reed	Speaker, U.S. House of Representatives
	Max. O'Reill	French Commentator and Humorist
1895	Thomas Dixon Jr., D.D.	Author and Lecturer
	Hon. Lemuel Ely Quigg	Member of Congress, Journalist
1896	A.J. Palmer, D.D.	Doctor of Divinity
	Hon. Theodore Roosevelt	Police Commissioner of New York
1897	St.Clair McKelway, LL.D.	Editor, "Brooklyn Eagle"
	Hon. James H. Eckles	U.S. Comptroller of Currency
1898	John H. Converse	President, Baldwin Locomotive Works
	Hon. Justin H. McCarthy, M.P.	English Commentator
1899	Cyrus T. Brady, D.D.	Author and Lecturer
	Maj. Gen. Nelson A. Miles	General, U.S. Army
1900	Hon. William A. Stone	Governor of Pennsylvania
	Hon. Grover Cleveland	Former President of the United States
1901	Col. Henry Watterson	Editor, Louisville "Courier Journal"
	Hon. Charles E. Smith	U.S. Postmaster General
1902	Clement A. Griscom	President, International Mercantile Marine
	Hon. Marcus A. Hanna	U.S. Senator from Ohio
1903	William A. Shanklin, LL.D.	President, Wesleyan University
	Hon. Leslie M. Shaw	Secretary of U.S. Treasury
1904	Hon. James M. Beck	U.S. Solicitor General
	Gen. Horatio C. King	Author and Lecturer
1905	E.T. Stotesbury	Head of House of Drexel and Company
	Hon. J.P. Dolliver	U.S. Senator from Iowa
1906	Hon. Charles J. Bonaparte	U.S. Attorney General
	Job E. Hedges, Esq.	Jurist, Member N.Y. Bar
1907	Hon. Champ Clark	Speaker, U.S. House of Representatives
	John K. Bangs	Lecturer and Humorist
1908	Bishop Luther B. Wilson, D.D., LL.D.	M.E. Bishop
	Hon. William J. Bryan	U.S. Secretary of State
1909	John Wesley, D.D.	Doctor of Divinity
	Hon. Charles Dick	U.S. Senator from Ohio
1910	David J. Burrell, D.D.	Doctor of Divinity
	Charles J. Goodell, D.D.	Doctor of Divinity
1911	Hon. John Wanamaker	Former Postmaster General
	Hon. Claude A. Swanson	U.S. Senator from Virginia, Sec'y. Navy
1912	Hon. Alba B. Johnson	President, Baldwin Locomotive Works
	Hon. Theodore E. Burton	U.S. Senator from Ohio

1913	Hon. John K. Tener	Governor of Pennsylvania
	Hon. William H. Taft	Former President of the United States
1914	Hon. George G. Orlady	Justice, Supreme Court, Pennsylvania
	Hon. William E. Borah	U.S. Senator from Ohio
1915	John Gribbel	President, Union League of Philadelphia
	Hon. Philip P. Campbell	Member of Congress
1916	Hon. George S. Graham	Member of Congress
	Gen. Leonard Wood, M.D., LL.D., D.Sc.	General, U.S. Army
1917	William D. Lewis, Ph.D.	Dean, Univ. of Pennsylvania Law School
	Hon. Theodore Roosevelt	Former President of the United States
1918	Michael F. Doyle, Esq.	Member, Philadelphia Bar
	Hon. Thomas R. Marshall	Vice-President of the United States
1919	Hon. J. Hampton Moore	Mayor of Philadelphia
	Hon. Josephus Daniels	Secretary, U.S. Navy
1920	Samuel M. Vauclain, Sc.D.	President, Baldwin Locomotive Works
	Hon. Julius Kahn	Member of Congress
1921	Cheesman Herrick, Ph.D., LL.D.	President, Girard College
	Hon. Charles E. Townsend	U.S. Senator from Michigan
1922	Hon. Hayyr S. McDevitt	Judge, Common Pleas, Philadelphia
	James S. Montgomery, D.D.	Chaplain, U.S. Senate
1923	Glen L. Swiggett, Ph.D.	U.S. Bureau of Education
	Hon. James M. Beck	Member of Congress
1924	Hon. William H. Shaffer	Justice, Supreme Court, Pennsylvania
	Hon. Harry S. New	U.S. Postmaster General
1925	Hon. Robert von Moschzisker	Justice, Supreme Court, Pennsylvania
	Hon. Dwight F. Davis	U.S. Secretary of War
1926	Josiah H. Penniman, LL.D., Litt.D.	Provost, University of Pennsylvania
	S. Parkes Cadman, D.D., S.T.D., D.H.L.	Doctor of Divinity
1927	Hon. Franklin S. Edmonds	Member, Pennsylvania Legislature
	Hon. Frank B. Willis	U.S. Senator from Ohio
1928	Hon. Harry A. Mackey	Mayor of Philadelphia
	Hon. Joseph T. Robinson	U.S. Senator from Arkansas
1929	Hon. Harry A. Mackey	Mayor of Philadelphia
	Hon. Charles Curtis	Vice-President of the United States
1930	Philip J. Steinmetz, S.T.D.	Doctor of Divinity
	Hon. Simeon D. Fess	U.S. Senator from Ohio
1931	Edward J. Cattell, D.Sc.	City Statistician, Philadelphia
	Hon. Daniel O. Hastings	U.S. Senator from Delaware
1932	Wilmer Krusen, LL.D., D.Sc.	Pres., Philadelphia College of Pharmacy
	Cheesman A. Herrick, Ph.D., LL.D.	President, Girard College
1933	Hon. J. Hampton Moore	Mayor of Philadelphia
	Hon. John Cornwell	Former Governor of West Virginia
1934	Hon. Roland S. Morris, LL.D.	Former U.S. Ambassador to Japan
	Hon. Donald R. Richberg	Executive Director, N.R.A.
1935	Hon. Otto R. Heiligman, LL.D.	Judge, Common Pleas, Philadelphia
	Mark Sullivan, A.B., LL.D.	Author and Columnist
1936	Hon. Harry A. Mackey	Ex-Mayor of Philadelphia
	Samuel K. Ratcliffe	British Journalist
1937	Michael F. Doyle, LL.D.	Member, Philadelphia Bar
	Hon. Alben W. Barkley	U.S. Senator from Kentucky
1938	Hon. Allen M. Stearne	Judge, Orphans Court, Philadelphia
	Harry A. Hopf	Management Engineer
1939	Hon. John W. Kephart	Chief Justice, Pennsylvania Supreme Court
	Dr. Frank Bohn	Author and Publicist
1940	Robert T. McCracken	Member, Philadelphia Bar
	Alexander Kerensky	Former Premier, Republic of Russia
1941	Hon. James G. Gordon Jr.	Pres. Judge, Common Pleas No.2
	Hugh Gibson	Diplomat and Publicist
	From 1942 to 1945, the period of World War II, Peirce School held no public commencement.	
1946	Michael F. Doyle, LL.D.	Member, Philadelphia Bar
1947	Bishop W.P. Remington, S.T.D.	P.E. Diocese of Philadelphia
1948	John R. Wanamaker	Merchant
	R. Adm. J.E. Wood, SC, USN	Naval Aviation Supply Officer
1949	Hon. Vincent A. Carroll, LL.D.	Judge, Common Pleas, Philadelphia
	Hon. William L. Batt, Sc.D.	Industrialist

1950	Morris Wolf, LL.B.	Member, Philadelphia Bar
	Walter D. Fuller, LL.D., Litt.D.	Publisher
1951	Clement V. Conole, B.S.	Exec. Dir., Philadelphia Chamber of Commerce
	R. Adm. S.E. McCarty, SC, USN	Aviation Supply Officer
1952	Hon. Harry V. Dougherty	Former Registrar of Wills, Philadelphia
	Hon. John S. Fine	Governor of Pennsylvania
1953	Hon. Harry V. Dougherty	Former Registrar of Wills, Philadelphia
	Hon. James A. Farley	Former U.S. Postmaster General
1954	Hon. Harry V. Dougherty	Former Registrar of Wills, Philadelphia
	Hon. James A. Duff	U.S. Senator from Pennsylvania
1955	Charles G. Reigner, Litt.D., LL.B.	Educational Author, Publisher
	Hon. Calvin D. Johnson	Former Member, U.S. Congress from Illinois
1956	William H. Evans, A.M.	Exec. V.P., Nat'l. Office Mgt. Assn.
	James E. Gheen	Inspirational Philosopher, Humorist
1957	Charles U. Shellenberger, A.B., LL.D.	Gen. Sec'y., YMCA, Philadelphia
	Andrew Mutch, D.D.	Doctor of Divinity
1958	Rev. B. Janney Rudderow, B.A.	Episcopal Priest
	Benjamin Fine, Ph.D., LL.D.	Journalist, Educator
1959	Rev. Robert S. Lowndes, B.A., B.D.	Educator
	Earl S. Rudisill, M.A., Ph.D.	Educator
1960	Rev. Howard G. Hartzell, A.B., B.D., Th.M.	Baptist Minister
	Carmela DeMarco and George A. Miller	Graduates
1961	Rev. Frederick J. Stevenson	Roman Catholic Educator
	Janet B. Belinsky and James H. Rogers	Graduates
1962	Rev. Terry R. Smith	Methodist Minister
	Cynthia J. Armstrong and Anthony J. Barry	Graduates
1963	Walter R. Hagey, LL.B., S.T.D., LL.D.	Banker
	Martha A. Trainer and R. Stevenson Scott Jr.	Graduates
1964	Lester F. Johnson, Ed.Sc.D.	Pa. Dept. of Public Instruction
1965	Harrison F. Dunning, A.B.	Industrialist
1966	Kenneth G. Matheson, B.S., M.A., Ph.D.	Educator
1967	Donald G. Barnhouse Jr., A.B., B.D.	News Analyst
1968	Richard R. Schweiker, B.A.	U.S. Congressman
1969	Herbert Gezork, Ph.D., D.D., LL.D.	Theologian
1970	John R. Bunting, B.S., M.A., D.B.A.	Banker
1971	Bernard N. Thorpe, B.A., B.D.	Lutheran Minister
1972	Bowen C. Dees, A.B., Ph.D.	Physicist
1973	John T. Gurash, Sc.D.	Corporation Executive
1974	R. Anderson Pew, B.S., M.S.	Corporation Executive
1975	Frederick Heldring, B.S.	Bnaker
1976	Mort Crim, A.A., B.Ed., M.S., Litt.D.	News Analyst
1977	Hon. Lisa A. Richette, B.S., LL.B.	Judge, Common Pleas, Philadelphia
1978	George Plimpton, B.A., B.A., M.A.	Writer, Editor
1979	Lynmar Brock Jr., A.B., M.B.A.	Entrepreneur
1980	Charles F. Dougherty, B.S.	U.S. Congressman
1981	John K. Nevin	Business, Civic Leader
1982	George Gilder	Economist, Author
1983	Hon. Lynne M. Abraham, B.A., J.D.	Judge, Common Pleas, Philadelphia
1984	Hon. W. Wilson Goode, B.S., M.G.A., LL.D.	Mayor of Philadelphia
1985	Robert E. Brennan, B.S., LL.D.	President, First Jersey Securities
1986	Kevin M. Tucker, B.A.	Philadelphia Police Commissioner
1987	Patricia T. Carbine, B.A.	Publisher, Editor
1988	Richard D. Wood, Esq.	President & Chief Executive Officer, Wawa Inc.
1989	Nelson G. Harris	President & CEO, Tasty Baking Company

Appendix B
Abbreviated Peirce Family Tree

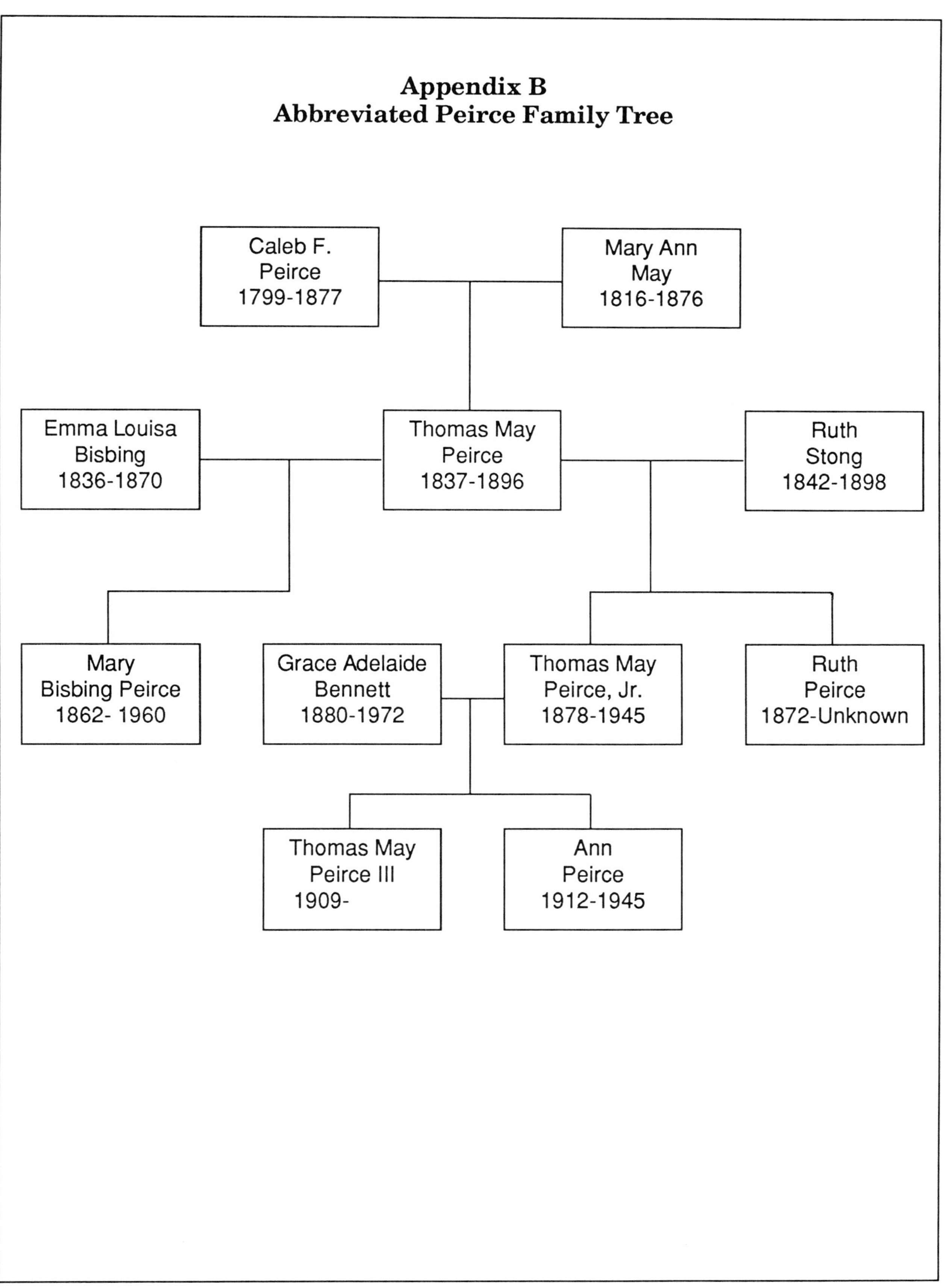